DATE DUE

MAY 0 8 2018			

#47-0108 Peel Off Pressure Sensitive

SOCIAL ISSUES
FIRSTHAND

Cancer

Other books in the Social Issues Firsthand series:

Cancer

Norah Piehl, Book Editor

GREENHAVEN PRESS

An imprint of Thomson Gale, a part of The Thomson Corporation

GALE™

Detroit • New York • San Francisco • New Haven, Conn. • Waterville, Maine • London

Christine Nasso, *Publisher*
Elizabeth Des Chenes, *Managing Editor*

© 2007 The Gale Group.

Star logo is a trademark and Gale and Greenhaven Press are registered trademarks used herein under license.

For more information, contact:
Greenhaven Press
27500 Drake Rd.
Farmington Hills, MI 48331-3535
Or you can visit our Internet site at http://www.gale.com

LIBRARY OF CONGRESS CATALOGING-IN-PUBLICATION DATA

Cancer / Norah Piehl, book editor.
   p. cm. -- (Social issues firsthand)
   Includes bibliographical references and index.
   ISBN-13: 978-0-7377-3834-6 (hardcover)
   1. Cancer--Social aspects. I. Piehl, Norah.
   RC262.C2662 2008
   362.196'994--dc22

                                                         2007024136

ISBN-10: 0-7377-3834-0 (hardcover)

Printed in the United States of America
10 9 8 7 6 5 4 3 2 1

Contents

Chapter 1: Receiving the Diagnosis

Chapter 2: Seeking Therapy

Chapter 4: Surviving and Thriving

Foreword

Social issues are often viewed in abstract terms. Pressing challenges such as poverty, homelessness, and addiction are viewed as problems to be defined and solved. Politicians, social scientists, and other experts engage in debates about the extent of the problems, their causes, and how best to remedy them. Often overlooked in these discussions is the human dimension of the issue. Behind every policy debate over poverty, homelessness, and substance abuse, for example, are real people struggling to make ends meet, to survive life on the streets, and to overcome addiction to drugs and alcohol. Their stories are ubiquitous and compelling. They are the stories of everyday people—perhaps your own family members or friends—and yet they rarely influence the debates taking place in state capitols, the national Congress, or the courts.

The disparity between the public debate and private experience of social issues is well illustrated by looking at the topic of poverty. Each year the U.S. Census Bureau establishes a poverty threshold. A household with an income below the threshold is defined as poor, while a household with an income above the threshold is considered able to live on a basic subsistence level. For example, in 2003 a family of two was considered poor if its income was less than $12,015; a family of four was defined as poor if its income was less than $18,810. Based on this system, the bureau estimates that 35.9 million Americans (12.5 percent of the population) lived below the poverty line in 2003, including 12.9 million children below the age of eighteen.

Commentators disagree about what these statistics mean. Social activists insist that the huge number of officially poor Americans translates into human suffering. Even many families that have incomes above the threshold, they maintain, are likely to be struggling to get by. Other commentators insist that the statistics exaggerate the problem of poverty in the United States. Compared to people in developing countries, they point out, most so-called poor families have a high quality of life. As stated by journalist Fidelis Iyebote, "Cars are owned by 70 percent of 'poor' households.... Color televisions belong to 97 percent of the 'poor' [and] videocassette recorders belong to nearly 75 percent.... Sixty-four percent have microwave ovens, half own a stereo system, and over a quarter possess an automatic dishwasher."

However, this debate over the poverty threshold and what it means is likely irrelevant to a person living in poverty. Simply put, poor people do not need the government to tell them whether they are poor. They can see it in the stack of bills they cannot pay. They are aware of it when they are forced to choose between paying rent or buying food for their children. They become painfully conscious of it when they lose their homes and are forced to live in their cars or on the streets. Indeed, the written stories of poor people define the meaning of poverty more vividly than a government bureaucracy could ever hope to. Narratives composed by the poor describe losing jobs due to injury or mental illness, depict horrific tales of childhood abuse and spousal violence, recount the loss of friends and family members. They evoke the slipping away of social supports and government assistance, the descent into substance abuse and addiction, the harsh realities of life on the streets. These are the perspectives on poverty that are too often omitted from discussions over the extent of the problem and how to solve it.

Greenhaven Press's Social Issues Firsthand series provides a forum for the often-overlooked human perspectives on society's most divisive topics of debate. Each volume focuses on one social issue and presents a collection of ten to sixteen narratives by those who have had personal involvement with the topic. Extra care has been taken to include a diverse range of perspectives. For example, in the volume on adoption, readers will find the stories of birth parents who have made an adoption plan, adoptive parents, and adoptees themselves. After exposure to these varied points of view, the reader will have a clearer understanding that adoption is an intense, emotional experience full of joyous highs and painful lows for all concerned.

The debate surrounding embryonic stem cell research illustrates the moral and ethical pressure that the public brings to bear on the scientific community. However, while nonexperts often criticize scientists for not considering the potential negative impact of their work, ironically the public's reaction against such discoveries can produce harmful results as well. For example, although the outcry against embryonic stem cell research in the United States has resulted in fewer embryos being destroyed, those with Parkinson's, such as actor Michael J. Fox, have argued that prohibiting the development of new stem cell lines ultimately will prevent a timely cure for the disease that is killing Fox and thousands of others.

Each book in the series contains several features that enhance its usefulness, including an in-depth introduction, an annotated table of contents, bibliographies for further research, a list of organizations to contact, and a thorough index. These elements—combined with the poignant voices of people touched by tragedy and triumph—make the Social Issues Firsthand series a valuable resource for research on today's topics of political discussion.

Introduction

Over the past half-century, breast cancer has been transformed from a highly stigmatized disease to one of the highest-profile health issues in this country. How did a disease once "utterly taboo"[1] become, according to a 1996 article, "This Year's Hot Charity,"[2] complete with well-publicized fundraisers, celebrity endorsements, and dozens of product tie-ins? Exploring this issue raises significant questions about cancer research and funding, charitable giving, and public health issues, and sheds some light on the complexities surrounding cancer in the United States in the early 2000s.

Excessive Attention?

Breast cancer is a serious disease, but it is neither the most common nor the most deadly form of cancer. According to the American Cancer Society[3], lung cancer was the leading cause of cancer death in the United States in 2006. An estimated 162,460 American died of lung cancer in 2006, compared to 41,430 deaths from breast cancer. There were an estimated 214,460 new cases of breast cancer in 2006, exceeding the number of lung cancer cases but fewer than the number of prostate cancer cases.

If funding for cancer research was based only on these statistics, one might expect it to be among the two or three forms of cancer that received the most research funding. In fact, scientists researching breast cancer received far more funding than those investigating other cancers, with more than $560 million in funding from the federal National Cancer Institute in 2005 (up from $155 million in 1992). By comparison research on prostate cancer was a distant second at $309 million, and there was no other type of cancer that received even half the funding that breast cancer did in that year.[4]

The Publicity Machine

One explanation for why breast cancer research receives a relatively high amount of funding is that breast cancer gets far and away the most media coverage of any type of cancer. According to a 2001 study, 61 percent of newspaper and magazine articles on cancer focused specifically on breast cancer, 23 percent on prostate cancer, 17 percent on colorectal cancer, and 9 percent on lung cancer (except for mentions of lung cancer in stories on the dangers of tobacco usage). The same study found that personal stories, such as the ones in this volume, were also heavily weighted toward breast cancer, representing more than 60 percent of published first-person narratives about cancer.[5]

Breast cancer's relatively high survivorship rate—the overall five-year-survival rate is 88 percent[6]—helps ensure that writings by and for breast cancer patients have a ready market. These personal narratives, both in print and online, have, in recent times, become almost unfailingly positive and optimistic. A recent article by singer Anastacia, diagnosed with breast cancer at the age of thirty-four, is a good example. "I now know that beauty isn't about having perfectly round breasts or a flawless complexion," Anastacia writes. "It's about who I am on the inside, and I have cancer to thank for that insight."[7]

The positive outlook of these survival stories is inspired, at least in part, by the breast cancer movement itself. In its early years, the modern breast cancer movement modeled itself on the highly successful AIDS awareness campaigns of the 1980s, even basing its widely recognized pink ribbons (originally distributed at Estée Lauder cosmetics counters in 1992) on the red ribbons associated with AIDS activism.[8] Breast cancer, however, had the distinct advantage of lacking any of the sexual and/or moral complexities surrounding the HIV/AIDS epidemic, and consequently the movement took off even more quickly, soon becoming the darling cause of celebrities and marketers alike. Witnessing the overwhelming success of the Estée Lauder campaign (more than 1.5 million ribbons were distributed the first year)[9], other companies also developed ways to tie into the breast cancer fundraising movement. In the early 2000s, consumers can collect pink lids from yogurt cartons, purchase commemorative postage stamps, or buy themed athletic shoes, lipstick, or lingerie, all to raise funds for breast cancer research and awareness campaigns.[10]

Critics of these brand-driven promotions, as well as of high-profile fundraising events such as the Susan G. Komen Race for the Cure and the Avon Breast Cancer 3-Day walks, point to the often minimal percentage of donations to these causes that actually go toward research, when weighed against the heavy costs of advertising and administration. The political group Breast Cancer Action sponsors a series of public awareness ads entitled "Think Before You Pink," arguing that these commercial campaigns exploit women's desire to support breast cancer causes but ultimately enhance corporate profits more than they do cancer research.[11] Organizations such as Breast Cancer Action urge women to return to political action, rather than consumerism, if they are interested in making real inroads in the fight against breast cancer. Critic Ellen Leopold writes, "The emphasis on consuming as a way of raising money shopping for the cure—trades on the most conventional expectations of women rather than on their capacity for social action."[12] As Alice O'Keeffe notes, this type of consumerist philanthropy also accentuates the fact that breast cancer is not "a disease associated with poverty—in fact, it affects people from higher-income backgrounds more than the poor."[13] By marketing breast cancer causes to upper-middle-class women—those most able to purchase these pink-themed items—critics contend that these charities paint breast cancer as a solely upper-middle-class issue, overlooking opportunities to advocate politically for more effective services to medically underserved women, such as minorities and the poor whose survivorship rates are significantly lower than those of white, middle-class breast cancer patients.[14]

The Role of Celebrities

Further underscoring both the consumerist aspects of the current breast cancer movement as well as its optimism is the role of celebrities in the fundraising campaigns. Almost from the beginning of the movement in the early 1990s, well-known, glamorous figures such as Ralph Lauren and Evelyn Lauder have been at the forefront of publicity efforts. What's more, media stories often focus on relatively young celebrity breast cancer survivors such as Kylie Minogue, Anastacia, and Sheryl Crow when they mention the disease, although, as Diana Jupp, a spokesperson for Breast Cancer Care, points out, young women represent a "tiny minority" of actual breast cancer cases.[15] Regardless of statistical sense, though, the very public battles of these famous, attractive women—not to mention the countless other female celebrities who have adopted breast cancer as a favorite charity—have done a great deal to raise the profile of the disease.

Celebrity faces of other cancers have had a harder time lobbying support for their causes. Notwithstanding the examples of famous cancer survivors Scott Hamilton and Lance Armstrong and the efforts of billionaire philanthropist Michael Milken, men's cancers, in particular, have remained in breast cancer's shadow. Prostate cancer organization names like "Us TOO" reflect the frustration of those trying to raise funds and awareness for these diseases. Debra Goldman reasons that unlike breast cancer advocates, these organizers may have trouble creating a real men's cancer movement reliant on corporate branding: "If you want a man to bond with your brand, reminding him that his penis may be a ticking time bomb is not the way to go about it."[16]

What About Other Cancers?

Men's cancers certainly have an image problem, as does a disease such as lung cancer, which still suffers from its connection to smoking, resulting in victim-blaming and stigmatization. The number one risk factor for breast cancer, on the other hand, is simply being female,[17] giving the breast cancer movement a formula for success that is free from any value judgments or shame. What's more, this shared risk offers women a ready opportunity for sisterhood, whether it be in the checkout line or on the race course.

Regardless, though, these highly publicized breast cancer efforts leave people with many questions to consider. Is it possible that the extremely successful breast cancer publicity machine is detracting much-needed public attention and funding from deadlier or more widespread cancers? Does the breast cancer movement's focus on early detection cause unnecessary fears, especially among younger women? Does the consumerist focus of some breast cancer advocacy efforts help or hurt the long-term prospects for federal cancer funding and for helping medically underserved women? And, finally, do the many achievements of the breast cancer movement—from raising funds to connecting survivors—outweigh concerns about its methods? Only time will tell—breast cancer activism may have started as a fashion trend, but unlike hemlines and hairstyles it's certainly here to stay.

Notes

1. Ellen Leopold, *A Darker Ribbon: Breast Cancer, Women, and Their Doctors in the Twentieth Century.* Boston: Beacon Press, 1999, p. 2.
2. Lisa Belkin, "Charity Begins at . . . The Marketing Meeting, The Gala Event, the Product Tie-In," *New York Times Magazine,* December 22, 1996.
3. American Cancer Society, "Cancer Facts and Figures," 2006.
4. National Cancer Institute, *Fact Book,* 2005. http://fmb.cancer.gov/financial/attachments/FY-2005-FACT-BOOK-FINAL.pdf
5. Summarized in "Media Coverage Trails Other Cancers," *USA Today (Magazine),* February 2001.
6. American Cancer Society, "Cancer Facts and Figures," 2006.
7. Anastacia, "How Breast Cancer Made Me Stronger," *Shape,* October 2006.

8. Samantha King, *Pink Ribbons, Inc.: Breast Cancer and the Politics of Philanthropy*. Minneapolis: University of Minnesota Press, 2006, p. xxiv.
9. King, *Pink Ribbons*, p. xxv.
10. Ellen Leopold, "Shopping for the Cure," *American Prospect*, September 25–October 9, 2000, pp. 15–17.
11. Breast Cancer Action, www.thinkbeforeyoupink.org. The Web site also includes a "Parade of Pink" directory of all product tie-ins for the breast cancer movement.
12. Leopold, "Shopping for the Cure," p. 17.
13. Alice O'Keeffe, "What Good the Pink Ribbon?" *New Statesman*, November 1, 2004, p. 26.
14. American Cancer Society, *Cancer Facts & Figures*, 2004; King, *Pink Ribbons, Inc.*, p. xviii.
15. Quoted in O'Keeffe, "What Good the Pink Ribbon?" p. 26.
16. Debra Goldman, "Illness as Metaphor," ADWEEK, November 3, 1997, p. 70.
17. Lisa Belkin, "Charity Begins at . . ."

SOCIAL ISSUES
FIRSTHAND

CHAPTER 1

Receiving the Diagnosis

The Fear of Not Knowing

Eliza Wood Livingston

Although other cancers such as breast, lung, and prostate cancer have benefited from large-scale campaigns to raise public awareness, cancer of the colon is still often treated as a topic of shame and embarrassment. Colorectal cancer is one of the leading causes of cancer deaths, but the disease is frequently not part of routine screenings and is often misdiagnosed.

Eliza Wood Livingston was diagnosed with stage III (advanced) colon cancer in 1996. In this essay, she describes the frightening experience of undergoing agonizing abdominal pain and other troublesome symptoms for more than a week before receiving her diagnosis. Livingston's story reflects not only the panic and fear that can accompany undiagnosed cancer but also the ways in which colon cancer's symptoms can be misdiagnosed, dismissed, and even ridiculed.

Prior to her diagnosis with colon caner, Eliza Livingston was a certified nurse-midwife in the obstetrical department of a major hospital in San Jose, California. Using her medical knowledge, Livingston wrote Living with Colon Cancer, *a book that both tells her own heroic story and offers tips for others undergoing similar struggles.*

The waiter sets down a plate on which is artfully arranged a fillet of wild salmon, a hillock of wild rice, a bundle of bright spring asparagus, and two orange nasturtiums with purple streaks blazing from their centers. The enticing arrangement of the food strikes a starkly dissenting note with the growing turmoil in my belly. Earlier I sampled the fried calamari with skordalia sauce. Perhaps the richness has thrown my bowels into this chaos. Yet, contrary to expectation, the cramping has not been relieved by a trip to the bathroom.

Listlessly pushing the food around my plate, I sip San Pellegrino in the hope that it might magically calm my stomach. Before the waiter can remark on my barely touched plate, I catch his eye and ask, "Could you wrap this up for me so I can take it home? This is all delicious, but I'm just not hungry." He studies my face briefly, smiles, and nods in agreement.

By Friday, three days later, the pain have become more intense, rolling over and through me in waves, eerily similar to the contractions of labor. I have been unable to eat since Tuesday, and drinking is becoming more difficult. Charles has made daily trips to the pharmacy, returning with Fleets enemas, castor oil, and citrate of magnesia. These serve only to increase the amplitude of the pain.

Charles insists on driving me the thirty miles to work that evening. Soothed by the steady hum of the car, I carefully stretch back and shut my eyes as we loop through the mountain roads.

Charles ventures, "Are you sure you should be doing this?"

"I'll be OK." Offering reassurance that I myself doubt, I am perplexed that this pain has lasted so long, that it is not abating with time. Yet in some way it feels as if a mysterious puzzle were lodged in my belly; I have only to find the key to discover its secrets, and then everything will return to normal. As I walk toward the double doors of the hospital, Charles calls out, "I'll pick you up anytime!" I turn and nod, smiling to reassure him. "Thanks, honey. I'll call you later."

Return to Work

The navy cotton scrubs I slip into have "Eliza Livingston, CNM," embroidered in deep burgundy floss across the pocket. Next, I pull on clean, high, white sneakers and tie my hair back with a silver barrette shaped like a lazy figure eight. Dropping two pens into the pocket of the scrubs, I throw on a white lab coat, push open the double doors marked "STOP:

LABOR AND DELIVERY: AUTHORIZED PERSONNEL ONLY," and walk out to the OB floor.

I make rounds on my patients, reviewing their prenatal charts, labs, progress notes, nursing notes, and orders. After seeing one patient, and before seeing the next, I retreat to the call room, take some deep breaths as the pain washes through me, and try to compose myself. Minutes later, poised and smiling, I return to the labor-and-delivery unit to resume periodic patient evaluations.

The laboring women work diligently to prepare their bodies for delivery, responding with sighs, groans, and shrieks to the rise and fall of the contractions grabbing their bellies. They are immersed in the holy agony that heralds the arrival of a tiny infant into waiting hands and arms and hearts. And I, too, labor with intense pain, pain that, like theirs, overwhelms me in rhythmic waves, subsiding only when I feel I can stand it no longer. Comforting them at the same time that their contractions are being mirrored within my own body is surreal.

The staccato *tap-tap-tapping* of the fetal heart makes irregular squiggles on the narrow strip of paper that flows from the squat gray machine at the side of the bed. A laboring mother named Luisa is dozing, released just now from the embrace of the last contraction. Sitting down on the bed, I absentmindedly stroke her legs.

The low grunts that she makes at the peak of her contraction suggest that she will be ready to deliver soon. I check her cervix: eight centimeters and paper thin. "You'll soon have a baby in your arms," I say. Smiling, I sit with her through another contraction. "You are doing such a good job!" During the lull before the next one I explain, "It's not time to push yet. If you really feel you can't help it, try blowing out in little puffs, as if you're blowing out a candle, and keep doing that until the urge passes." She watches me inhale deeply and then exhale in a rhythmic fluttering of shallow pants. She nods, inhales, and slowly lets out the air in light staccato breaths. "Good, Luisa. I'll be back in a few minutes. You're on the home stretch!"

Pausing for Pain

Stepping out to the hall, I walk down to the OR scrub area, take a mask and high paper boots from the shelves, and put them on the delivery table outside Luisa's room.

It is ten-thirty. Since arriving only three hours ago, my patients' labors have progressed, and the pain in my own gut has intensified, rolling over me in waves, before slowly ebbing.

I inform the clerk at the nurses' station that I'll be back in the call room for a few minutes, and I hurry out of the unit. After crawling carefully onto the narrow bed, I curl around my belly. The pain pulls at me, pulls me up to lean against the wall. Finding no relief, I bend over like a jackknife being squeezed closed, grabbing my ankles tightly. Panting, I stifle the groans that form in my throat. Rivulets of sweat run down my neck and face.

Is there a meaning to this pain that leaves me pleading for mercy? I know only that no baby will be my reward for this struggle. . . .

When the pain subsides, I dial the MD call room and try to sound offhand. "I'm having some stomach problems; I'm OK now, but I just want to let you know that I may have to go down to the ER later to get checked out."

"If you feel sick, go to the ER now; there is no reason to wait." There is a pause before the doctor speaks again. "I'll cover the floor.". . .

In the ER

"Eliza Livingston!" A nurse in worn green scrubs gestures for me to follow and ushers me into a narrow cubicle. Below the striped canvas curtains hanging from metal shower hooks, I can see the feet of people moving about in the adjoining cubicles. There is barely space to walk around the bed. As a nurse, I have passed rows of beds such as these, each one offering an illusion of privacy. The air thickens with the murmur of low voices punctuated by exclamations of pain, the intimate sounds of bodily functions responding to disease, and tired voices reciting the litany of discharge orders. The nurse hands me a wrinkled gown printed with pale tan flowers and snaps at the shoulders.

A harried doctor rushes in and asks a few brief questions: "When did your pain start? What medications have you taken?" Between the pulsations of pain, I tell him that I have been unable to eat since Tuesday and unable to drink since yesterday. I add that I have not had a bowel movement in three days, that I have tried enemas and citrate of magnesia, and that neither has relieved the cramping or constipation.

He absently notes my responses as he listens to a message from a disembodied voice behind the curtain, "Patient in 1C allergic to penicillin; what do you want to give her?"

He orders the voice to give ceftriaxone.

"And start an IV on this patient. Give her seventy-five of Demerol [a painkiller]."

The scratch of pen on paper pauses, and he nods in my direction. "And we'd better get some abdominals [x-rays] on her, too." And then he is gone.

To the X-Ray Room

Scant minutes pass before the nurse returns with a warm blanket and a loaded syringe. I watch her jam the needle into the port of the IV tubing and slowly push the plunger. Feeling the Demerol sweep over me, releasing the tension in my body and offering respite from the relentless pain, I float into a light sleep.

The doctor returns and repeats some of the same questions. I wince as he presses into my belly.

"Ten years ago I had surgery for a bleeding ulcer; can this pain be from surgical adhesions [scars]?"

"Maybe," he pauses. "We'll get some films of your abdomen just to check it out."

I snooze again while waiting for the orderly to take me to x-ray, and I continue to doze as he pushes me through the halls. The radiology technician asks me to get down from the gurney and stand against the film plate. He helps me to the floor, but I am unable to stand straight, and I slide from side to side against the plate. "Stand straight and tall, straight and tall." I know what he wants; I just can't do it. I open my eyes but am unable to focus—the entire room spins like a carousel on uneven ground, and the face of die diligent technician becomes a blurry swirl of features. I slump over the plate, and he agrees, "Well, I guess this is the best you can do . . . it's OK . . . hold still now." I hear the *thunk-chunking* sound signaling that I can move again, and I feel his arms helping me onto the gurney. Back in the curtain-lined cubicle, I sleep.

"The x-rays are normal." The doctor's voice startles me. "You can go home now, but come back if the pain persists. I'm sending you home with some pills you can take for the pain." He disappears, and I fall into a dreamless sleep. . . .

Sent Home

The cramps start again that evening as the Demerol wears off. My abdomen feels bloated and hard. I am unable to eat or drink. In my pocket, I find the Ziploc bag containing the pills that were given to me last night. The label reads "Hydrocodone bitartrate 5 mg with acetaminophen 500 mg. Take 1–2 tabs every 4–6 hours." Another note, "Take with food," has been scratched out. Fearing that narcotics will serve to mask whatever is going on and very likely exacerbate it, I put the pills aside. When I shuffle to the bathroom, I notice that my urine is meager in volume and the color of ripening apricots.

My son Andrew calls but, too tired to speak or even to think clearly, I pass the phone to Charles. Andrew is an internist and a cardiology fellow at Scripps. I can hear Charles struggling to describe what has happened at the ER and can feel his frustration at trying to answer Andrew's questions.

"Yeah, I will," Charles nods into the phone before handing it back to me.

"Mom, you need to see a surgeon. Go back to the ER, and don't let them send you home until you see a surgeon. OK?"

"OK." I feel embarrassed to be making a fuss about constipation and a bellyache. . . .

Return to the ER

When we get to the hospital, [This is the author's third visit to the ER.] I am ushered into the exam room and told to sit on the narrow table. After the medical assistant takes my blood pressure and temperature, the doctor walks in. "I'm Dr. Douglas. So what's happening with you?" he asks. Once again, I begin to tell my story.

He interrupts, chuckling, "You've just been eating too much ice cream lately!" He presses gently on my abdomen; it resists the slightest depression. "Don't be embarrassed. That's one of my weak spots, too." I haven't mentioned ice cream and can't remember when I last ate any. Lying on the exam table, listening to his glib diagnosis of ice cream gluttony, I feel as if I am floating through the looking glass with Alice.

He looks down on me, and the image of his face merges with the dream priest looking down on me before slashing crosses in my abdomen. "Well, just to be sure it's nothing else, let's order a flexible sigmoidoscopy [an examination of the rectum and lower colon using a flexible tube]."

"When?"

He replies casually that he will send a referral and that someone will call in the next few weeks to make an appointment. As he walks toward the door, I ask feebly, "In the mean-time, what about this pain and constipation?"

"Oh, take some milk of magnesia," he casually replies.

"How much?" Near tears, I can't believe that this visit is ending without resolution. "How often?"

He is in the hallway now and leans against the doorway as he directs, "One tablespoon every six hours until you have a bowel movement." He smiles broadly, playfully shaking his finger at me. "And no more ice cream!" Years later, I read his notes on this visit, which conclude, "NAD, bowel sounds nor-mative, and mild distension."

"Something Is Terribly Wrong"

Worn out from the relentless pain, I stumble into the waiting room and fall into Charles's arms. Leaning heavily into the ample refuge of his chest, I stagger down the hall and through the courtyard to the parking lot. He drives smoothly and care-fully, yet I am carried into every twist and turn of the moun-tain road and feel every bump and jostle.

Crawling into bed back at home, I curl around my aching belly, but I am unable to find a position that is tolerable. Charles tries to help me settle before calling Andrew, but there is little he can do. Rolling from side to side in a futile attempt to dodge the pain, I can hear him saying into the mouthpiece, "OK. . . . OK."

Unable to smother my groans, I whisper to Charles, "I have to go back—I am in agony. Something is terribly wrong."

"I'm taking her back now," Charles says into the phone. "I'll call you."

Back on the curvy mountain road and back to the ER. Charles helps me into a wheelchair and pushes me to the ad-mitting window. I hold my card up to the hand reaching for-ward. Like an angry puppet popping up on a stage, a woman with furrowed brows and tight lips leans over the counter and snaps, "What did you come back here for? You should have called an advice nurse. That's what they're for, to take care of things like this over the phone!" I am too astonished to reply.

Eventually I am wheeled into an exam room, Charles following closely. I see Dr. Metzger [another ER doctor] walk past the open door and shut my eyes. I hear him take a chart out of the rack, flip through the pages, sigh, and walk in. "Well, you're back. Don't you remember, I said that many times we never know where abdominal pain comes from—we just never know."

"I remember that," I apologize, "but the pain, it's indescribable. Something feels terribly wrong"

Doubting Myself

He looks at Charles, rolls his eyes, and shrugs. Charles tells him that Andrew wants me to be evaluated by a surgeon. He also notes that Andrew has spoken to one of the staff internists, who wants to be called. Metzger raises his eyebrows in surprise. "If I decide that, in my judgment, she needs to be seen by a surgeon or an internist, I'll call one."

Then he looks at me skeptically and suggests that I have been taking pain medicine. [Dr. Metzger had told her pain medicine would worsen a bowel blockage.]

Exasperated, Charles sputters, "She hasn't had any pain medicine! She hasn't had anything to eat or drink for days. Nothing!"

Dr. Metzger appears to doubt our report. He decides to take more abdominal films, and again, he interprets them as normal. "Well, we may never know the cause of this pain," he repeats. "You know, most of the abdominal pain that comes through the ER—we never know what causes it!"

His inability to make a diagnosis is not surprising, given that he has done so little to figure out the etiology [reason] of my symptoms.

I am puzzled that, although I have been seen repeatedly over a period of three days for persistent abdominal pain, no one has done either a pelvic or rectal exam.

Even his evaluation of my taut abdomen has been cursory and inattentive. And I suspect that he might be misinterpreting the x-rays. I wonder whether he has consulted with a radiologist. He coaxes me to doubt my memory: Perhaps it hasn't been so long since I have had a bowel movement? And surely, I have tried some pain medications . . . haven't I?

A "Simple" Diagnosis

Again, he decides that dehydration is the problem and orders an IV.

"But . . . there must be something behind the dehydration," Charles stammers. "What's wrong that she can't drink? That she's so dehydrated? That she—"

The doctor interrupts, "She's dehydrated because she's not drinking." His voice lifts in triumph. "It's that simple!"

Toward midnight, at the end of the doctor's shift, he sends a nurse in to disconnect the IV and prepare me for discharge. Discharge teaching includes instructions for the BRAT diet: bananas, rice, applesauce, and toast. I know this diet. It is prescribed for patients with diarrhea. "I do not have diarrhea." The tears are swelling in my throat. "I *wish* I had diarrhea!" Flustered, the nurse flees from the room.

Suddenly, my stomach heaves and, leaning through the metal side rails of the bed, I yell for help. I vomit viscous dark yellow fluid into the murky pink basin that is pushed in front of me. A different nurse is attached to the hand that holds the basin. She touches my hair, offers me a clean towel, and murmurs words of comfort. That tender touch, that voice of compassion from this luminous being kindles in my heart a wavering flame of hope.

Charles asks the doctor who just came in with the new shift about getting a surgical consult. "We only call a second doc if it is, in our opinion, necessary. There is no reason to request a surgical consult for your wife. This is probably just dehydration, and when she gets her flexible sig, that will rule out anything more serious." He ambles out of the cubicle.

A Secret Ally

Convinced that this is far more serious than "simple dehydration," I am becoming increasingly frightened. I know that I can no longer think clearly. The days of pain and exhaustion have left me weak and rudderless, a wounded ship adrift on a treacherous sea. "Something is so terribly wrong," I whisper. "I think I am dying." I feel the nurse's calm hands smoothing my hair.

"Yes. I know. You need to stay. I tried to tell him but . . ." She shrugs helplessly. "I'll just take a long time getting you ready to go."

This gracious and discerning woman has looked at me and seen the anguish that no one else seems able to appreciate. My secret ally.

Moaning, I lean between the steel bed rails. More dark yellow bile shoots out of my mouth onto the gray linoleum squares. "I'm sorry. I'm so sorry."

"It's OK. I just didn't get the basin to you in time." The nurse gently draws a cold, wet cloth across my face and props a clean basin by the pillow. Feeling safe for the first time since this siege began, I want her never to leave me.

A Fresh Pair of Eyes

"Hi." A hesitant voice drifts toward me. "Hi. My name is John. I am a fourth-year medical student. Can I ask you some questions?"

A towheaded fellow in green OR scrubs, clutching a clipboard and pen, John stands some distance from the bed as he waits for my response.

"Oh, God, something is terribly wrong."

"I just have to ask you a few questions, and then the surgeons will come in to see you." He hesitates, waiting for encouragement. I am unable to offer any, yet my heart leaps at his mentioning that surgeons are on their way. He draws a deep breath and asks, "When did your pain start?"

"Tuesday."

"Oh, that's seven days!" He hesitates. "Can you describe the pain?"

"Hmmm. It's agony," Hating to let him down, I try to be more precise. "It's rhythmic. Stabbing."

He scribbles onto the clipboard. "And can you tell me what you've done for it?"

"Oh, oh . . . here it comes again." I curl around my belly. "Fleets. Citrate. . . ." The coil of pain wrapping around my bowels leaves me speechless.

He waits quietly until the contraction passes and I uncoil myself.

"When was your last bowel movement?"

"Last Monday."

"Hmm." He taps his pen against the paper pad on the clipboard. "When was your last period?"

"Due tomorrow actually." A deep moan shudders through my body as another pain reaches its zenith.

"That's OK," he pats my shoulder hesitantly. "I'm going to get the surgeon."

"Thank you." Seeing the fear in his eyes, I want to smile, to reassure him, yet my attention and energy are spent. His footsteps fade. A paradox, I think to myself, this young man just beginning his training appears to see a truth that eludes staff physicians with years of experience tucked under their belts.

A Surgical Perspective

"Mrs. Livingston!" I hear a clipped British accent. "Mrs. Livingston. Can you open your eyes?" Moaning acknowledgment,

I look up. The face is narrow. Dark eyes shine behind steel-rimmed spectacles. "My name is Dr. Narayan. I am the surgical resident." . . .

"I know you've told your history far too many times to far too many people already, so I'll just say that we need to open you up to see what's causing all this trouble." He pauses, as if waiting for my response. "I'm afraid we have no alternative," he apologizes. "The x-rays strongly suggest a blockage in the large bowel." *The x-rays that Dr. Metzger insisted were normal*, I think to myself. I am not surprised. . . .

No Time to Waste

Dr. Narayan writes some orders on the chart and hands it to the nurse at his side. Asking my permission, he carefully pulls back the bed sheet to expose my abdomen. He gently touches the skin, noticing the heat, the boardlike rigidity, the distension. "Ah, yes, we need waste no time."

A tall man with a gentle concern in his eyes approaches the bedside and looks down into my face. Dr. Narayan speaks again. "This is Dr. Zang. He will be the main surgeon, and as I said, I'll assist."

Dr. Zang looks at me kindly. "We don't know what's causing this blockage: It could be adhesions from your prior surgery. But whatever it is, we need to operate without delay." He touches my shoulder reassuringly. "We'll give you something for the pain and nausea right away and be getting you ready for surgery at the same time."

I close my eyes. What incited these angels of mercy to materialize at my bedside? After days of being dismissed by doctors and staff eager to reduce their ER load, I am being heard.

A Roller-Coaster Diagnosis

Marjorie Williams

"I've hated roller coasters all my life," writes Marjorie Williams in her essay. Finding a diagnosis for cancer, however, is like the ultimate roller coaster, alternating between the highs of hope and the depths of fear and despair. In Williams's case, the final diagnosis was dire indeed—at the age of forty-three, she learned she had Stage IV (untreatable) liver cancer, with possibly only months to live.

Understandably, Williams's account focuses on her own fears and uncertainties as well as her family history (her father suffered from cancer) and her family's future, as she worries about what will happen to her two young children. Despite her prognosis, in this writing, Williams remains pragmatic and even optimistic in the face of the scariest roller coaster of all.

Marjorie Williams was a columnist for the Washington Post, *contributing political profiles and other essays to the newspaper. Following a nearly four-year battle with liver cancer, Williams died in January 2005. Her husband, also a journalist, later published many of her political and personal writings in a collection titled* The Woman at the Washington Zoo.

The beast first showed its face benignly, in the late-June warmth of a California swimming pool, and it would take me more than a year to know it for what it was. Willie and I were lolling happily in the sunny shallow end of my in-laws' pool when he—then only seven—said, "Mommy, you're getting thinner."

It was true, I realized with some pleasure. Those intractable 10 or 15 pounds that had settled in over the course of two pregnancies: hadn't they seemed, lately, to be melting away? I had never gained enough weight to think about trying very hard to lose it, except for sporadic, failed commitments to the health club. But I'd carried—for so many years I hardly noticed it—an unpleasant sensation of being more cushiony than I wanted to be. And now, without trying, I'd lost at least five pounds, perhaps even eight.

I suppose I fell into the smug assumption that I had magically restored the lucky metabolism of my 20s and 30s, when it had been easy for me to carry between 110 and 120 pounds on a frame of five feet six inches. True, in the months before Willie's observation, I'd been working harder, and more happily, than I had in years—burning more fuel through later nights and busier days. I'd also been smoking, an old habit I'd fallen into again two years earlier, bouncing back and forth between quitting and succumbing, working up to something like eight cigarettes a day.

A Warning in Disguise

Of course Willie noticed it first, I now think: children major in the study of their mothers, and Willie has the elder child's umbilical awareness of me. But how is it that I didn't even question a weight loss striking enough for a child to speak up about? I was too happy enjoying this unexpected gift to question it even briefly: the American woman's yearning for thinness is so deeply a part of me that it never crossed my mind that a weight loss could herald something other than good fortune.

As it happened, I took up running about a month later, in concert with quitting smoking for good. By the end of the summer I was running about four miles a day, at least five days a week. And with all that exercise I found I could eat pretty much anything I wanted without worrying about my weight. So more weight melted away, and the steady weight loss that might have warned me something was going badly wrong disguised itself instead as the reward for all those pounding steps I was taking through the chill of early fall, the sting of winter, the beauty of spring's beginning. I went from around 126 pounds, in the spring of 2000, to about 109 a year later.

Somewhere in there my period became irregular—first it was late, then it stopped altogether. Well, I'd heard of this: women who exercise heavily sometimes do become amenorrheic [without menstruation]. I discussed it with my gynecologist in January, and he agreed it was no real cause for alarm. He checked my hormone levels and found I definitely hadn't hit perimenopause [transitional time around menopause], but what I most remember about that visit is the amazed approval with which he commented on the good shape I was in.

Finding a Lump

Around that time—I can't pinpoint exactly when—I began to have hot flashes, almost unnoticeable at first, gradually increasing in intensity. Well, I said to myself, I must be perimenopausal after all; a gynecologist friend told me that hormone levels can fluctuate so much that the test my doctor had done wasn't necessarily the last word on the subject.

Then one day in April I was lying on my back, talking idly on the telephone (strangely, I don't remember to whom), and running my hand up and down my now deliciously scrawny stomach. And just like that I felt it: a mass, about the size of a small apricot, on the lower right side of my abdomen. My mind swung sharply into focus: Have I ever felt this thing before, this lump? Well, who knows, maybe this is a part of my anatomy I was just never aware of before—I had always had a little layer of fat between my skin and the mysteries of the innards. Maybe there was some part of the intestine that felt that way, and I had just never been thin enough to notice it before.

You know how you've always wondered about it: Would you notice if you had a sudden lump? Would you be sensible enough to do something about it? How would your mind react? For all of us, those wonderings have a luxuriantly melodramatic quality. Because surely that isn't really how it works; you don't just stumble onto the fact that you have a lethal cancer while you're gabbing on the phone like a teenager. Surely you can't have a death sentence so close to the surface, just resting there, without your being in some other way aware of it. . . .

"I would think," he [Williams's general physician] said, "that what you're feeling is stool that's moving through your bowel. What you're feeling is a loop of intestine or something where the stool is stuck for a while. That's why sometimes it's there and sometimes it's not. The bad things don't come and go; the bad things only come and stay." He could send me off for a lot of tests, he said, but there really wasn't any point in going to that trouble and expense, because I was so obviously a perfectly healthy patient. He repeated all the same information in a letter mailed to me the following week after my blood tests came back: Healthy healthy healthy.

Looking back, I know I was uneasy even after I got this clean bill of health. Sometimes I sensed what seemed like a flicker of movement in my belly, and got the oddest feeling that I might be pregnant. (At one point, I even bought a home pregnancy test and furtively took it in a stall in the ladies room in the little mall that housed the pharmacy.) Every now and then, the mass in my abdomen actually stuck out when I lay on my back: once, I looked down to see my stomach distinctly tilted-high on the right side, much lower on the left. I was at some pains never to point this out to my husband, Tim.

Finally, on the last Friday night in June 2001, I had a huge hot flash while my husband was tickling my back, in bed. Suddenly I was drenched, I could feel that his fingers could no longer slide easily along the skin of my back. He turned to me, astonished: "What is this?" he asked. "You're covered in sweat."

Slowing Down, Noticing Things

It was as if someone had at last given me permission to notice fully what was happening inside me. I made an appointment with my gynecologist—the earliest one I could get was the next week, on Thursday, July 5—and began deliberately noticing how overwhelming the hot flashes had gotten. Now that I was paying close attention, I realized they were coming 15 or 20 times a day, sweeping over and through me and leaving me sheathed in a layer of sweat. They came when I ran, making my joyous morning run a tedious slog that must be gotten through; they came when I sat still. They exceeded anything that had been described to me as the gradual coming of menopause. This was more like walking into a wall. On both Monday and Tuesday of that week, I remember, I stopped about two miles into my morning run, simply stopped, despite the freshness of the morning and the beauty of the path I usually cut through the gardened streets of Takoma Park. Any runner knows the feeling of having to push past the body's observation that it might be more fun to walk slowly home and pop open a beer (just keep putting one foot in front of the other), but this was something different, like an override system I could no longer ignore. It said: Stop. It said: This is a body that can no longer afford to run.

My gynecologist's office is way, way out in the long exurban belt stretching westward from D.C. Pat was running late that afternoon, so it was probably after five when he finally called me into his office. I told him about the hot flashes, and about the lump I was feeling in my abdomen. "Yup, you're in menopause," he said somewhat brusquely. "We can start giving you hormones, but first let's check out that lump you say you're feeling."

We went into the examining room, where he keeps his ultrasound equipment. He'd given me dozens of quick exams with it over my childbearing years. I hopped up on the table, and he slapped on some of the chilly goo they apply to your belly, to make the ultrasound mouse slide over your skin, and almost immediately he stopped: "There," he said. "Yeah, there's something here." He looked at it a bit more, very briefly, then started snapping off his gloves. His face looked as neutral as he could possibly make it, which alarmed me instantly. "Just so you know," he said quickly, "it's probably fibroids. I'm not thinking cancer, but I am thinking surgery. So get dressed and come on back to my office, and I'll explain."

We sat back down on opposite sides of his desk. But before we talked, he called out to his receptionist, who was just packing up for the evening. "Before you go," he said, "I need you to book her an ultrasound and a CT [computed tomography—a type of diagnostic imagery] scan. Tomorrow, if possible."

I told Pat he was scaring me: what was all this speed about if he wasn't thinking cancer? . . .

Learning to Be a Patient

As a patient, you come to feel that you need everyone—from the chairman of the ontology service at a major cancer center down to the least-paid clerk in the admissions department—to like you. Some of them may have the power to save your life. Others have the power to make you comfortable in the middle of the night, or to steer away from you the nurse-in-training who is still just learning to insert IVs, or to squeeze you in for a test you might otherwise wait days for.

I was discovering this truth on my back, while the ultrasound technician guided her wand through the chilly gel she had squeezed onto my belly. She was a friendly young woman with a Spanish accent of some kind, and her job was to get an accurate picture of what was going on in my pelvis while divulging the least information possible to the anxious patient. My job was to find out as much as I could, as quickly as I could.

So there I am: "Gosh, Friday afternoon . . . Have you had a long week? . . . How long have you been working in ultrasound? . . . Oh! Is that my ovary there, really? . . . Ah, so you're taking pictures now . . . Uhhuh . . . Gee, that must be the growth my gynecologist was talking about."

Troubling Ultrasound

Under this onslaught of niceness, the technician begins to think aloud a bit. Yes, she is seeing a growth. But usually fibroids, which grow from the outside of the uterus, move in concert with it: poke the uterus and the growth will move too. This growth seemed to be independent of the uterus.

Is it a mild chill I'm feeling, or a mild thrill? I am still reeling at the thought that I might have a hysterectomy at 43; perhaps I am thinking it would at least be fun to have something more interesting than a fibroid?

But if there is a tinge of that interest, it vanishes when she speaks again: "Huh. Here's another one." And another. Suddenly, we are seeing three strange round plants that yield to a mild shove, but don't behave like anything she's ever seen before. She is doubly skeptical now about the fibroid theory. My gynecologist had examined me in detail the previous January, so much of what we're looking at has to have grown within six months. Fibroids, she says, don't grow nearly that fast.

I am surprised that she is so forthcoming, but soon see that it is of little use to me: she is looking at something she's never seen before. She summons the doctor—the chief radiologist in the practice—who in turn summons a younger colleague she is training. They all crowd around the machine in fascination.

A Chilling Certainty

Again, we do the poking-the-uterus exercise. We try the transvaginal sonography wand. Their mystification has begun to make me seriously frightened. I begin to question the doctor very directly. She is quite kind. She really can't say what she's seeing, she tells me.

It almost seems an afterthought—the indulgence of a hunch—when the doctor turns to the technician and says, "Try moving up, yes, to the navel or so." I can still remember the feel of the equipment casually gliding up toward my navel, and then a sudden, palpable tension in the air. For, immediately, another large growth—one even bigger than the three below—looms into view.

This is the moment when I know for certain that I have cancer. Without anyone's even looking very hard, this exam has been turning up mysterious blobs in every quarter. I go very still as the doctor begins directing the technician to turn here, look there. Her voice has dropped almost to a whisper, and I don't want to distract her with my anxious questions: I can hold them long enough for her to find out what I need to know.

But then I hear one of them mumble to the other, "You see there? There is some ascites [abnormal build up of fluid] . . . ," and I feel panic wash through me. Along with my sisters, I nursed my mother through her death from a liver illness, and I know that ascites is the fluid that collects around the liver when it is badly diseased.

Suspecting Cancer

"Are you finding something on my liver too?" I croak.

"Yes, something, we're not sure what," says the doctor, pressing a sympathetic hand to my shoulder. And then suddenly I'm aware that they've made a decision to stop this exam. What's the point in finding more? They've found out enough to know that they need the more subtle diagnostic view of a CT scan.

"Is there a case to be made against my freaking out now?" I ask.

Well, yes, replies the doctor. There's a lot we don't know; there's a lot we need to find out; it could be a great range of different things, some of which would be better than others.

"But then let me ask you this way," I press. "Do you know of anything other than cancer that could give rise to the number of growths we just saw? Could it be anything benign?"

"Well, no," she says. "Not that I'm aware of." . . .

Finally, Diagnosis

[During the next week, the author undergoes a CT scan and a biopsy.] Dr. Goodguy [nickname for the surgeon] calls about three p.m. He has a Very Serious Doctor Voice on, and jumps right in: "Well, this isn't good. It's not lymphoma. Your pathology report shows that your tumor is consistent with hepatoma, which is, uh, which is liver cancer." Already I am struggling: does "consistent with" mean they think that but they don't really know it? No, those are just scientific weasel words they use in pathology reports. (A pathologist, I will learn, would look at your nose and report that it is consistent with a breathing apparatus.)

I know this diagnosis is very, very bad. Liver cancer is one of the possibilities I researched in my compulsive tours of the Internet over the weekend, so I already know it's one of the worst things you can have. Still, I say to the doctor, "Well, how bad is that?"

"I won't avoid it. It's very serious."

"And it would presumably be bad news that it's already created other tumors around my body?"

"Yes. Yes, that is a bad sign."

A lovely man, who's doing a hard job with a patient he just met three days before. There are at least five large metastases of the cancer in my pelvis and abdomen, and the mother ship—a tumor the size of a navel orange—straddles the channel where the major blood vessels run into and out of the liver. Tumors so widespread automatically "stage" my cancer at IV(b). There is no V, and there is no (c).

Sharing the News

When I hang up the phone I call Tim and tell him. We make it as clinical a conversation as possible, because otherwise there will be so much feeling it might stand in the way of acting. He is on his way home, right away.

I call my friend Liz and tell her. I tell her some of the statistics—that, as I read the data, I may be dead by Christmas. Liz almost always says the perfect thing, from the heart, and now she says the two things I most need to hear. The first is "I want you to know that, whatever happens, I will be with you the whole way."

The second is "And you know that all of us—but this is my promise—we will all work to keep you alive in your children's minds." Now tears are pouring down my cheeks, and they feel good.

Indulging Curiosity

The drama of discovery and diagnosis happened so long ago, and has been followed by so many drastic plot twists, that it feels to me like ancient history. But I've noticed that almost everyone I talk to is very curious to know those details. Whenever the whim of disease takes me into the view of a new doctor or nurse, we fall into the standard, boring rhythm of summarizing history and condition (when diagnosed; at what stage; what treatments have been administered since, with what results). If the person I'm talking to is young and relatively inexperienced, I may find myself more schooled in this procedure even than she or he is. But there always comes a moment when their professionalism suddenly drops, their clipboards drift to their sides, and they say, "Uhn, how—do you mind if I ask you how you happened to find out you had cancer?" I realize at these times that they are asking as fellow humans, not too much younger than I am, and their fascination is the same as everyone else's: Could this happen to me? How would I know? What would that feel like?

We have all indulged this curiosity, haven't we? What would I do if I suddenly found I had a short time to live . . . What would it be like to sit in a doctor's office and hear a death sentence? I had entertained those fantasies just like the next person. So when it actually happened, I felt weirdly like an actor in a melodrama. I had—and still sometimes have— the feeling that I was doing, or had done, something faintly self-dramatizing, something a bit too attention-getting. . . .

Living on Borrowed Time

In two months I will mark the finish of year 3 b.t.—my third year of Borrowed Time. (Or, as I think of it on my best days, Bonus Time.) When I was diagnosed with Stage IV(b) liver cancer in early July of 2001, every doctor was at great pains to make clear to me that this was a death sentence. Unless you find liver cancer early enough to have a surgeon cut out the primary tumor before it spreads, you have little chance of parole. The five-year survival rate for those who can't have surgery is less than 1 percent; my cancer had spread so widely that I was facing a prognosis somewhere between three and six months. I was 43; my children were 5 and 8. . . .

I live at least two different lives. In the background, usually, is the knowledge that, for all my good fortune so far, I will still die of this disease. This is where I wage the physical fight, which is, to say the least, a deeply unpleasant process. And beyond the concrete challenges of needles and mouth sores and barf basins and barium, it has thrown me on a roller coaster that sometimes clatters up a hill, giving me a more hopeful, more distant view than I'd expected, and at other times plunges faster and farther than I think I can endure. Even when you know the plunge is coming—it's in the

nature of a roller coaster, after all, and you know that you dis-
embark on the bottom and not the top—even then, it comes
with some element of fresh despair.

I've hated roller coasters all my life.

But in the foreground is regular existence: love the kids,
buy them new shoes, enjoy their burgeoning wit, get some
writing done, plan vacations with Tim, have coffee with my
friends. Having found myself faced with that old bull-session
question (What would you do if you found out you had a
year to live?), I learned that a woman with children has the
privilege or duty of bypassing the existential. What you do if
you have little kids is lead as normal a life as possible, only
with more pancakes.

My Wife Has Breast Cancer

Brendan Halpin

When Brendan Halpin's wife Kirsten was first diagnosed with breast cancer, she urged her husband to cope with his feelings by keeping a journal. Frustrated by the lack of memoirs written by the partners of women with breast cancer, he took his wife up on the idea. Halpin's journal entries, in addition to detailing Kirsten's diagnosis and treatments, also provide an honest, in-depth glimpse into his doubts and fears—emotions he can't even admit openly to his wife. Halpin's writing is candid and often raw, revealing his anger and feelings of helplessness as well as reflecting on issues of masculinity, marriage, and fatherhood.

Brendan Halpin is a writer and teacher who lives in Boston, Massachusetts. His wife Kristen, the subject of his breast cancer Memoir, It Takes a Worried Man, *died in 2003. Halpin has also published three novels and another memoir about teaching.*

Waiting to See a Specialist

The ultrasound came back inconclusive. The doc said something like, "It doesn't really look cancerous. It doesn't really look benign." Apparently it was round on one side, which is cystlike, and nubbly on the other side, which is cancerlike. So they set up an appointment with a surgeon who is some kind of breast specialist.

Weeks went by, as they always do when you are waiting to see a specialist. We unpacked, worked on the new house, stripped wallpaper, and made a million trips to the Home Depot.

The breast specialist looked at the ultrasound and decided to order a mammogram and a "needle biopsy." Here's where it started to get scary. But okay, you can still talk to ten women and probably five of them have had an ultimately benign lump in their breast biopsied.

I didn't go with her to the biopsy. It didn't seem important. It's just a formality. When they described the procedure to her, they said it was basically sticking a needle into the lump and sucking some cells out.

A Bruising Biopsy

When she came home, her breast was bandaged, bruised, and bloody. She described how they had held this gun-like apparatus to her breast and fired it in nine times. They sent her home with this information sheet that said, "You may experience some oozing." All of a sudden, this felt real. I got incredibly sad when she undressed. It just looked like she'd been beaten up. I guess she had. I had to leave the room to cry, because I understood very clearly that my role was to be positive. This looked bad, though.

The biopsy was Friday morning before Labor Day weekend, so it was going to be Wednesday before we found anything out. We had dinner with some friends and had a very nice weekend....

Facing Bad News

I carry a pager, but I have it in my pocket on this day. We don't let the kids [Halpin's students] carry them, and I sort of hate to have it on my belt proclaiming my hypocrisy of the adult world, so I keep it in my pocket. While I am walking to the bookstore, my pager vibrates, but because I am wearing these loose-fitting pants, I don't feel it.

I buy some pens and index cards. I head back to school in a leisurely way. I stop and talk to somebody in the faculty room. I eventually check my e-mail. I read and respond to about three messages. Then I open the one from the office manager, which says, "Your lovely wife has been trying to reach you. She is at the hospital. Please call her."

Well, that's it, isn't it? They only make you come to the hospital if they have bad news for you. They call you up and say, "Come in to discuss your results," because they don't want to tell you bad news on the phone, but of course they already have, because if they had good news, they would just say, "Your biopsy came back totally normal."

I duck into a room and call the number she's given me. It rings and rings and rings and rings. I call home—no answer. I call the hospital again. It rings and rings and rings. What the hell kind of hospital is this? Are there no receptionists? Is there no voice mail? This endlessly ringing phone just seems ominous. I am on the verge of tears.

And then I see her through the door. Kirsten has come to school to find me. I see her smile at one of my co-workers—maybe it's not terrible news after all. She comes in the room and begins to sob. "I have cancer," she says. I hold her while she cries. "I'm so scared. I don't want to die."

"You won't," I tell her. "You won't."

Scared of Losing Her

We talk for a few more minutes, then she goes out to the car, while I head back into the room I share with five other teachers to grab my backpack and jacket. Practically everyone in this room is new to the school. Luckily Lisa, whom I have known for a year, is there. She looks at me, and I am about to cry. "Is everything okay?" she asks, and I sort of pull her back to the corner of the room.

"Kirsten has cancer," I sob, and she hugs me. "I don't know what I'm going to do. I'm not strong enough to do this. I can't lose her. I can't lose her." Lisa says reassuring things about how I am not going to lose her and I have lots of help, so I don't need to be strong all by myself. It's true. She will see me cry many more times before the treatment even starts.

I gather my stuff and leave, and the other people I share the room with politely pretend that they haven't heard and they aren't curious. This is a great kindness.

A Plan of Action

The plan, Kirsten explains, is for her to have a semiradical or total or, anyway, some kind of mastectomy that involves hacking her entire breast, and then some, off. Then a little radiation, a little chemo, and boom, she's better.

Of course, I am already worried about her dying. As much as I reassure her, it is just in my hypochondriac nature to imagine the worst. All I can think is, "How will I get Rowen [their young daughter] to school?" and, "Oh my God, does this mean my mom will have to move in?"

She now needs to go for several tests to make sure the cancer hasn't spread. First they tell her she needs a bone scan. Then they say she needs a bone scan and a CAT [computed axial tomography; an imaging method] scan. But they hadn't said that two days ago. Are they acting on some new information?

Why yes, as a matter of fact, they are. When Kirsten is reeling from the radioactive shake they made her drink, she runs into her breast specialist surgeon outside the hospital. The surgeon tells her that her bloodwork came back a little abnormal. Two of the tumor markers are elevated. I don't know what this means. I later find out that tumors not in the breast cause some kind of elevated hormone levels in your blood, so this is bad news. And they told her on the f---ing street. . . .

"The Land of the Critically Ill"

It has been, to put it mildly, a real bitch of a week. On top of everything else, Kirsten had to take an indefinite leave from her job teaching refugees how to get and keep jobs in hotels. The money, luckily, is not an issue because our Troll-free home is a multifamily and the rents cover our mortgage, but it is a real psychological blow to both of us for her to have to stop working. Welcome to the Land of the Critically Ill.

Doctor Sensitive, Ms. "Your Tumor Markers Are Elevated, Oh, There's My Bus," calls on Friday night. She says to Kirsten, "I think there was some mistake in your bloodwork. If your potassium level is this high, you should already be dead. I'm sure it's a mistake, but you need to go to the emergency room right away and have it retested."

I had really been looking forward to kicking back with a beer and a sporting event, but it was not to be. I had also been looking forward to a calm, uneventful year of working on the house and the yard. But what the hell are you going to do.

Talking to My Daughter

So off we go to the emergency room. I drop Kirsten off and Rowen and I head off to this amazing and really cheap Mexican place about ten minutes' walk from the hospital. On the way over to dinner, I end up talking to Rowen about what's happening, about how Mom is going to have surgery (I show her my appendectomy scar to sort of illustrate the concept of surgery) and then she'll need to come back to the hospital for treatment, and how that will involve her getting some really strong medicine that is going to make her feel crappy for a while but will eventually make her better.

I get through this okay, though I almost start to cry when I realize that some passer-by is listening to us. We get to the restaurant and eat outside and watch people heading over to the Red Sox game. It's a practically perfect night. We go to the playground across the street after dinner. As strange as it sounds, it is a wonderful, wonderful night.

Letting Ourselves Laugh

We walk back to the hospital and find Kirsten in an examining room behind the emergency room. She seems to be in pretty good spirits. "The doctor's name is Nancy Drew [the heroine of a series of 1930s detective novels]," she whispers to me after the emergency room doctor walks out. "I haven't made any girl-detective jokes. I was very tempted to ask her about Ned, but I decided I didn't want to annoy her." I would never be able to be so strong. But keeping quiet is the best course of action. What kind of Nancy Drew joke do you think you could come up with that she hasn't already heard?

So Nancy Drew comes in and says the lab boys have their shorts all bunched up and don't understand how this happened and want to study Kirsten's blood as some kind of freak of science, but basically her potassium level is fine, her heart hasn't stopped, she's not dead.

Then she says, "Do you have any other health problems?"

We both laugh. Nancy Drew looks hurt, but I keep laughing. It is the funniest thing I have heard all week.

The Multi Disappointment

Somebody calls Kirsten and says, "You have a multi disappointment on Thursday." She eventually figures out that this is oncology lingo for "multidisciplinary appointment." The first reading seems a lot more in line with everything we've experienced so far. It is to be a two-hour appointment, and I get out of work right at the end of school so as to make the second hour.

I could have probably left earlier and made the first hour too, but that would have involved getting a sub for my afternoon class. Leaving work in any way cuts into my little wall of denial, and I hate that. I like going to work and just forgetting that anything is happening.

The multi disappointment really really blows. We sit in the f---ing room for really long periods of time waiting for people to show up. The radiation guy is incredibly lugubrious. He makes all these vague statements, like, "Well, of course, if the cancer has spread, as we think it may have because of these test results, then the objective of the treatment changes." Well what exactly the f--- does that mean? If the objective of the treatment is currently to save her life, then what's the new objective?

The nurse, on the other hand, is extremely chipper. I want to smack her. We spend forty-five minutes waiting for Maryann, the oncologist, who is very nice and extremely attractive, and she tells us nothing new at all.

The thing that really pisses me off, that makes me want to slap the whole bunch of them, is the fact that they just can't hide it: fundamentally, they are scientists, and they want all their data to make sense. Right now they have one piece of data that doesn't make sense, and it's driving them nuts. They *want* it to have spread. That way their test makes sense. Bastards.

What the CAT Scan Said

The day after the multi disappointment, Kirsten is told that they found something on her CAT scan. It is a spot on her spine. They don't know exactly what it is.

This is not good news.

Kirsten is pretty much beside herself. She pages me, but I am already in the subway station. I am now wearing my pager on my belt and enduring the kids' taunts about my hypocrisy with stoicism and the occasional, "Lay off, because if I tell you why I have this, you're going to feel bad."

I call her up.

"Where are you?" she asks. I can tell by her tone of voice that something is wrong.

"I'm in the subway station."

"Okay, then just come home and I'll tell you when you get here."

"Is everything okay?"

"Just . . . just come home. I just had a bad conversation with Maryann."

It takes a very long twenty minutes to get home.

When I walk inside she starts to cry. I hold her, and she tells me that she is tired, just so tired of getting bad news. I am too. She is a little confused about the news—she sort of stopped processing after the initial information—so I call Maryann, the oncologist.

Talking with the Oncologist

Here are some highlights of our conversation:

"Well, we see this spot on one of her vertebrae. It could be something we call a bone island, which is something we see on CAT scans from time to time and we don't know exactly what they are and we only gave them a name because we kept seeing them on CAT scans."

This sounds like good news to me. I am getting hopeful.

"But," she continues, "this doesn't really look characteristic of one of those."

Shit. "Does it," I say, "look characteristic of cancer?"

"Well, no. We don't really know what it is. The MRI [magnetic resonance imaging] and the PET [positron emission tomography] scan should tell us for sure."

The PET scan does not find out if you should have a dog, by the way. It involves being shot up with radioactive glucose, which tumor cells for some reason like a lot more than regular cells, so when the technicians take some kind of picture of you, the tumor cells glow brighter. Or something.

Has the Cancer Spread?

She goes on to say that we are still assuming that she will have a mastectomy in a week and a half, but we will need to see from the results of the tests next week. If the tests show that the spot is cancerous, then the surgery is off, because, basically, what's the point. See, it turns out that breast cancer in the actual breast never kills anybody. Makes sense, because if you needed breasts to live, they couldn't very well cut them off. It's only when it gets out that it kills you, usually by going after your liver. So if Kirsten's is out of the barn, so to speak, there is no sense in trying to shut the gate and "the objective of the treatment changes."

I decide to go for the big question. "So if this is metastatic [spread throughout the body]," I say, "is that a death sentence? Because that's what we're hearing."

Beat.

Beat.

Beat.

A "Very Special" Patient

I have prepared meals in less time than it takes for her to answer this. "Well," she starts out, "there are some very special patients—I mean, we are talking about the Louis Armstrong of cancer patients—" This analogy annoys me somehow. I don't know why. Couldn't she say the Michael Jordan of cancer patients? Maybe the Eddie Van Halen of cancer patients? The, um, Pedro Martinez? I don't know. I am not very familiar with Satchmo's oeuvre, so I find this annoying. "—who respond very well to treatment and can live relatively normal lives for years."

"When you say that the objective of the treatment is different, what exactly do you mean? Are we talking about pain abatement, or are we talking about fighting the disease?"

"Oh, we are absolutely fighting this disease," she says emphatically. I think she is horrified that I suggested that they sounded like they were giving up after they basically said they were giving up for two days. She goes on to say that while this would be bad news, it would be the best bad news possible, since these spots are tiny, and she has nothing wrong with her liver. Somehow I manage to come away from the conversation with the idea that she could live ten years with this treatment. I figure if ten, why not twenty or thirty? You are always hearing about these people: "The doctors told her she had a year to live, and twenty-five years later, she is fine . . ." I write a quote from Maryann in big letters in the cancer notebook: BAD BUT FIGHTABLE. I feel optimistic. Sort of. . . .

A Shocking Question

At some point during the initial weeks, Kirsten turns to me and says, "So are you going to have an affair?" I just have nothing to say except, "No. Why on earth would you say that?"

I am flabbergasted not because she's read my mind but because having an affair is probably the furthest thing from my mind. I work next to a large university, and I walk through campus before and after work on the way to the subway. I always enjoy ogling the undergraduate cuties, but after Kirsten's diagnosis I am sort of repulsed by the twenty-year-olds in their skintight tank tops. All I can think is, "Jesus, look at them lugging those cancer bags around."

So Kirsten's inquiry strikes me as really odd. She follows up with, "They say a lot of men do." And I am once more embarrassed to be a man. What kind of jackass runs around on his wife at a time like this? This comes after the initial diagnosis period when every medical professional she came in contact with seemed mildly surprised to find that she had a "supportive husband." She said they told her, "a lot of men aren't."

Why Men Do It

I can't help but feel contempt for these guys. What the hell do you think your marriage is if you can't support your wife when she's fighting for her life? I just sort of imagine these guys being like, "Okay, good luck with the mastectomy, hon, I'll be playing golf."

Well, it only takes a few days before I understand the jackasses a little better. I am back to ogling the undergraduate cuties, and while I am not about to have an affair, I sort of understand why men do it. Wouldn't it be nice to have something in my life that was just easy and fun? Right now everything is really really hard, and even the fun stuff seems to have a cloud over it. (Yes, I imagine knowing that you were cheating on your critically ill spouse might cast a pall over the adulterous proceedings, but I guess you never know.)

Emotional Deception

I also understand how people do it. I have always thought that I would be a horrible adulterer—basically she would know the second I got home because I am a terrible liar. But I am getting better. In fact, for the first time in my life, I am engaged in a large-scale pattern of deception, hiding huge chunks of my emotional life from Kirsten. I am usually unable to hide anything, to a degree that gets annoying, but now I am worried all the time, I am incredibly sad, I am terrified of losing her, but I can't let any of this stuff show at home. I have to be positive, because *she* has to believe that she can beat this disease, and in order for her to believe this, I have to believe it. And I do. But there is a whole other side of my life that I now must conceal.

So should I ever decide to have an affair, I now possess one of the essential skills. I have learned how to lie to my wife.

I sort of hate to go home at the end of the day now. At work, I can just worry about work, and I am trying to mediate these ridiculous conflicts about who said what about whose boyfriend, and then I have to go home and face the reality of what's happening. And the reality really really sucks. I don't play golf, but if I did, I might go for a few rounds right about now.

SOCIAL ISSUES
FIRSTHAND

CHAPTER 2

Seeking Therapy

Alternative Therapies
Saved My Life

Gabriella Messina

*In 1995, at the age of thirty-one, Gabriella Messina was diag-
nosed with lung cancer despite the fact that she had never
smoked. Following surgery to remove her right lung, Messina's
prognosis was discouraging, since it appeared the cancer had already begun to spread. Messina declined the recommended radiation treatments, instead choosing an aggressive alternative
regimen that included a complete diet overload, intensive herbal
and enzymatic supplements, and regular enemas.*

*Messina credits this program, along with yoga, meditation,
and traditional psychotherapy, with not only curing her cancer
but also encouraging her to adopt a more positive, productive
outlook on life.*

*Gabriella Messina is a freelance writer, actress, and media
producer.*

In 1995 I left my job as a television producer for ABC news.
I'd been battling colds, bronchitis, and a severe case of
pneumonia, and desperately needed relief from my stressful
job. I was planning to pursue a freelance career in television
and to reconnect with my passion for singing and acting.

But sitting in my naturopathic [an alternative therapy
based on preventive, holistic care] physician's office two
months after leaving my job, I coughed and bright red blood
spewed from my mouth. I almost fainted from fear. My doctor put me in a cab to the nearest emergency room, but I
stopped at a friend's birthday party instead—because I'd
promised that I would.

I was at the party only a few minutes before friends rushed
me to the hospital. Tests revealed a large malignant tumor

growing up my right bronchial tube, leaching into my lung and the outer lining of my heart. It was a form of cancer known as adenoid cystic carcinoma.

Screaming for Help

Surgeons removed the tumor and, along with it, my right lung. But a biopsy revealed that the cancer had already spread into some surrounding lymph nodes. My oncologist recommended several weeks of radiation therapy, despite its limited success rate against my type of cancer and the possibility of damage to my remaining lung. "Without radiation," he said, "you're looking at a 50 to 60 percent chance of recurrence."

As he went on describing the pluses and minuses of the therapy, every cell in my body protested. I told him the treatments were not for me.

Frightened as I was, I read everything I could about my illness. I felt I had to know why this had happened to me. I was only 31 years old at the time. I ate well and exercised and had never smoked. In books by mind-body gurus Louise L. Hay and Caroline Myss, Ph.D., I finally found some answers. I learned that I wasn't simply a victim of a malign fate but that I'd played a role, however unconsciously, in creating my illness. Deep down, I realized that to heal from cancer I would have to restore not only my physical body, but also my mind and my spirit, because all three had been wounded.

Repairing My Body

My first priority was my body, and I started looking for a doctor who specialized in cancer and nutrition. As fate would have it, a friend reminded me of an article I'd clipped in November of 1991 from *Natural Health* about a New York City doctor, Nicholas Gonzalez, M.D., who'd had promising results treating cancer patients with a nutritional regimen. I'd kept the article in a file of stories I wanted to produce for television, but now it might save my life.

Just seven weeks after my surgery, I was in Dr. Gonzalez's office, feeling hopeful. He explained that his treatment is based on three components: an individualized organic diet; a detoxification regimen, which includes twice-daily coffee enemas; and massive quantities of vitamins, minerals, and pancreatic enzymes. These enzymes, which aid digestion, are the crux of his program. His theory is that in high quantities they "digest" cancer cells, too.

His protocol meant a lifestyle change, and it didn't come cheap, especially since my health insurance refused to pay for any of it. The office visits, the organic food, and the supplements would cost me more than $1,000 a month for the rest of my life. But the regimen felt pleasantly familiar. It reminded me of how my Sicilian grandmother had treated my childhood illnesses with homemade herbs and tonics.

Beginning the Program

I began the program with a liver flush and colon cleanse, followed by a two-day juice fast. Then I added supplements and food. A typical day started at 6 a.m. with a coffee enema followed by 10 pancreatic enzymes. I took five more doses of these enzymes, including one at 3:30 in the morning, always without food. I envisioned the enzymes as Pac-Man figures swallowing the bad guys—in this case, the cancer cells. The rest of the supplements, taken with meals, brought me to a daily grand total of 135 pills. I would cycle off the pills after 15 days for a five-day break, and then I'd start again.

I adhered strictly to my prescribed almost-vegetarian diet, which consisted of raw organic produce (often juiced), whole grains, nuts, beans, and some fish, but no poultry, meat, refined sugars, or processed foods. It was socially restrictive and enormously time-consuming, but I believed that my life depended on it.

My three sisters and my parents cooked and shopped when I was too weak to do it myself. My partner found organic restaurants to take me to, and my 80-year-old aunt baked me special batches of Italian pastries with whole-grain flour, no sugar, and organic milk.

Healing My Mind and My Spirit

After I'd begun to heal my body, I was faced with the challenge of healing my inner self. To lower my stress level, I began to practice yoga and meditation. Then, with the help of a conventional therapist and an energy healer, I worked to acknowledge my anger and regret over failed relationships and over my long-abandoned dream of becoming a famous singer. I saw how my anxious striving for perfection and my controlling behavior had been driven by a fear of failure.

I learned that some healers believe that grief is stored in the lungs—where my cancer was—and I realized that I'd often resisted expressing painful feelings. The therapist and the healer made it possible for me to express them, and I cried a lot for the first six months after my diagnosis. But little by little, my sadness was replaced by a feeling of peace and a lightness of spirit, both of which had been sorely missing from my life.

Today I'm cancer-free. My remaining lung has expanded and I have better breathing capacity than the average person. I still see Dr. Gonzalez and follow the program—the diet, the detox regime (only one daily enema), and the supplements (down to no pills a day)—though I have to admit that I occasionally fall behind on my pills and my diet isn't always organic. I'm now living fully in every moment and creating the life I always wanted.

An Interview with a Life-Affirming Oncologist

Lisa Kogan

Oncology is a medical specialty with an extraordinarily high rate of burnout. The daily stresses of working with critically ill patients and their families can lead some oncologists to become emotionally distant, to avoid discussing any issues beyond the basic medical questions of diagnoses, prognoses, and treatments. An exception is Dr. Julia A. Smith, a passionate, hands-on oncologist who doesn't shy away from the tough questions.

Dr. Smith's patients work with her to decode complicated— and sometimes contradictory—advice, as well as to discuss difficult issues such as family dynamics, patient advocacy, and end-of-life care. Dr. Smith's patients remark on her positive attitude, which she passes on to her patients as well. In this interview, Dr. Smith explains how she can remain positive in the face of cancer and discusses how she views her role in working with her patients.

Dr. Julia A. Smith is a clinical assistant professor of oncology at the New York University School of Medicine. She is also the head of NYU's Breast Cancer Screening and Prevention Program. Her research interests include risk assessment, cancer screening, and early detection.

"She looks into your body and soul at the same time."

"She's like a brilliant medical detective. She studied my slides herself, cell by cell."

"She said, 'What do you want to do with the rest of your life?' I'll never forget that. Because if nothing else, it implied I still had more life."

"She asked the most amazing question: 'Do you have an intuitive sense of what's going on in your body?' Usually all anyone asks about is my insurance situation."

"She dropped by my apartment because she'd heard it was a walk-up and she wanted to be sure I could handle the stairs."

"She called on the Saturday before my surgery and said, 'I just want you to feel as good about yourself as I feel about you. You're going to do very well.' I was still facing this major operation, but I suddenly felt a tremendous burden had been lifted."

"She knows you're putting your life in her hands."

The "she" is Julia A. Smith, MD, PhD, a clinical assistant professor of medicine in the division of oncology at the New York University School of Medicine. But in private practice, as a doctor who provides consultations to patients trying to decipher the complicated issues surrounding cancer, she's just Julia. There are not a lot of Julias out there (more than one of the people quoted above expressed genuine regret that she can't be cloned). But in an attempt to pass along some of her practical magic, I visited her at Bellevue Hospital Center, where, in addition to her other work, she's helping to run a high-risk breast cancer screening clinic targeting the underinsured and underserved population of New York. There we talked about the day-to-day realities of coping with cancer: dealing with the medical world, giving and receiving support from close friends and anxious family handling fear, and living a vital and fulfilling life.

The Relationship Between Doctor and Patient

LISA KOGAN: What made you decide to do this?

JULIA SMITH: I'd get calls saying, I know you can't take any more patients but could you just see my sister, my mother, my friend, my son, because she or he has a diagnosis and doesn't know what to do, or doesn't understand what's being said, or understands but got two very different opinions, or has reached a branch point in treatment and must make a decision.

LK: Their own doctors couldn't help them?

JS: People don't get to spend time with their doctor—which is frustrating because most of us went into medicine wanting to be able to give real thought to each case. Often there's no absolute solution. Just as there's not one way to live a life. In determining what course to follow, we have to take the time to learn what's tolerable, how much uncertainty patients can handle, the constraints on their lives and their family, their economic situation, their work situation—then come up with a plan.

LK: Is that what you teach your medical students?

JS: We explore the relationship between doctor and patient. I tell my students that the great gift you get as a doctor is your patient. It's not that you licked this cell or you beat that tumor or you got remission partway here or completely there. It's the people who fill up your life. As a doctor you see in a very palpable way that in the end, life is really about the process.

An Upside to Cancer?

LK: Some of the process is very hard.

JS: When you have cancer you can't make the hard stuff disappear, but you can have something to do with how the process is played out. You get the chance to really focus on what you feel. Usually people have to get through middle age before even starting to—with some peace of mind—review their lives and come to terms with their choices.

LK: If there's an upside to critical illness, maybe that's it.

JS: You know, cancer takes so much away. From little things like the strength of your fingernails and the nature of your taste buds all the way to the ability to control your own destiny. But I hope what's gained is a true sense of self. You start asking what can and cannot be adjusted, what can and cannot be controlled. What do I want to be and what do I have to be.

LK: Everybody lives those questions daily.

JS: Yes, and with cancer you begin finding answers. Most of my patients tell me that they never would have chosen to get sick but they wouldn't give back what they've learned for anything.

LK: Julia, how do you stay strong? How do you keep their pain from wearing you down?

JS: Yes, well, that's hard, really hard. But the triumphs, and by that I don't just mean the out-and-out cures but the lives that are being lived fully and contentedly and gracefully—those things bring me great joy.

Advice for New Patients

LK: Once you're plunged into this parallel universe, is there some basic information you need right away?

JS: Often people get a diagnosis and feel they've got to have whatever the doctor recommends that day or the next. The fact is, tumors can take years to establish themselves. So unless there's a medical emergency, you have at least a few days to a few weeks to sit back and figure out exactly what you want to do.

LK: Do you encourage patients to bring a friend to appointments?

JS: Yes. The information is complicated and you're getting it at a time when you're probably pretty anxious. Of course when patients come with a lot of people and they all lump in, it only adds to the difficulty. . . .

LK: I'm picturing you with a megaphone and pie charts.

JS: [laughs] But having someone who will be there with you later is a good idea. And I encourage that person to call me, too.

LK: Really?

JS: Sure, because someone close to you is more likely to catch it if a patient is closing down or is too afraid to bring something up.

LK: I guess they're also bound to have feelings that need dealing with.

JS: There are issues like life support, pain management, home care versus hospitalization versus hospice care; there's the do-not-resuscitate order. Those are hard things to handle. I want to make relationships open enough so everyone's fears can be addressed. Because a loved one's fears are usually totally different from the fears of the person with the disease.

LK: Is being left behind high on the list?

JS: Yes, and that raises all kinds of other issues. It's tough, because loved ones are not the primary focus but they do have needs. You don't help if you just use them as an ancillary tool in a patient's care. They're not. They're a vital part of the patient's life.

LK: What else should patients be doing?

JS: I'd say make a list of things that worry you, things you don't understand, and don't be afraid if you can't articulate exactly what you want to say—everyone in medicine is used to that. Life-threatening illness requires learning a whole new vocabulary.

Alternative Therapies

LK: How do you feel about alternative medicine?

JS: If doctors had all the answers, I'd say don't investigate anything—just do what we tell you. But we don't have all the answers. And it's fundamentally healthy to search for help elsewhere. The problem is, if you don't have the science to back it up then you don't know what will actually help and what might hurt. There's an enormous desire to try to do something; there's often great pressure on doctors to act. But that's not always best.

LK: My friend tried an herbal remedy and spent election night wheezing in the emergency room. Of course she now claims it began when Tom Brokaw took Florida away from Al Gore.

JS: [laughs] I have no problem with things that aren't proven, provided they won't interact badly with other medication or prevent or delay treatment that we know could help.

LK: What about something like acupuncture or massage?

JS: At the very least acupuncture and other physical manipulations can have a soothing effect that shouldn't be minimized. But you have to see someone reputable and coordinate with your doctor.

Working with Children

LK: Let's shift gears. How involved should little kids be in the illness of a loved one?

JS: Having young children at a bedside when someone is dying could be more frightening than helpful to them. But maybe they should be in the garden outside the hospital, so they know they were there and part of it.

LK: Do you talk with people's kids?

JS: Almost always. The death of a sibling or parent will affect them through their whole lives. They need to ask questions that they can't ask people they're close to because they'll feel guilty expressing certain thoughts.

There's the initial impact, but also later, sometimes out of the blue, memories come crashing in on them. They need to know there's somewhere they can go to revisit the experience in an objective way. Generally, I think people are better off not trying to spare loved ones. But I'd never make that decision for a patient.

LK: They must be afraid their loved ones won't be able to handle serious illness.

JS: But you can't hide it from anyone who is truly involved in your life. If you try, they'll know something's wrong and feel totally excluded. They won't be able to offer whatever they could offer you—or what they need to offer for themselves, as a person who loves you. How your loved ones dealt with your illness will affect them forever. So if they mean something to you, deeply mean something, you might want to think about giving them a chance.

LK: And if it turns out that they actually can't deal with it?

JS: Then they'll indicate that, and you can find a way to make your peace with them. But whether you're grateful and pleased or you're disappointed and surprised, their reaction will teach you something. They may be close to you in ways you never imagined. They may not be close in ways you expected. And that's very valuable in understanding who you are and how your relationships have been formed.

Helping Patients Die

LK: How do you help a person die?

JS: With some patients that's what the whole treatment is about. With others it comes to that at some point. It's not like a massive heart attack. One minute you're thinking you're in your prime and the next you're thinking you may die. Cancer is a telescoping of life. You get the chance to explore all these things you wanted to explore—hopefully, by the time your body and mind and soul need to let go.

LK: What if a patient simply isn't ready?

JS: Then my job is to help them find a way to be ready when the time comes. Not to push them to be ready before they're ready. Sometimes the fight itself is critical and they need to continue the fight. But usually knowing you're doing everything you can to make your life as you wish it to be allows people to accept death. It's a question of helping patients find a way to hear their body saying it's okay to let go now, I have done enough, I have had a life, I have been here, and I don't have to fight for another minute.

LK: I wish we could all have these conversations while we're still healthy.

JS: Dying has an awesomeness, but there's also fear. People should be allowed to talk about that. And doctors should encourage these discussions. You don't have to be morbid or dwell on it. But facing death is part of the whole life cycle and talking about it should be part of treatment.

LK: Julia, you must cry all the time.

JS: Well, if you didn't have people in your life who you cared about, who meant enough to make you cry, then you wouldn't really have a life.

CHAPTER 3

Dying with Grace and Dignity

How to Say Goodbye

Eric R. Kingson

In 1998, Joan Kingson was diagnosed with colon cancer, which eventually spread to her liver. After a 32-month battle against the disease, Joan died in May of 2001. Here, her husband Eric shares an account of Joan's last week. Having exhausted all medical possibilities, Joan is free to say her good-byes to Eric, their two children, and the rest of their family and friends in peace.

Kingson's account of Joan's final days demonstrates the importance for terminally ill patients of remaining connected to family and of taking time to say farewells. In a particularly moving passage, Joan videotapes messages to those closest to her, messages that will always be cherished, particularly by her children. Kingson's story also illustrates the close relationships that can form between doctors, nurses, and patients during long struggles against cancer.

Eric R. Kingson is a professor in the School of Social Work at Syracuse University. His account of Joan's battle with colon cancer is entitled Lessons from Joan. *He and Joan were married for twenty-two years.*

Joan was relatively comfortable, in pretty good spirits, and enjoying time with Aaron [their son], Johanna [their daughter], Cathy [Joan's sister] and close friends. The nurses and aides thought she was pretty special. Here was a woman who in all probability was dying, yet she remained engaged in the life of her family and friends, in good humor, and even willing to engage staff in serious conversation. Still a teacher, Joan was always willing to allow medical and nursing students to be present during procedures and even during discussions about sensitive matters. I recall the gratitude of one nursing student who was invited to stay in the room when Joan's oncologist reviewed the relative merits of implementing a "do not resuscitate" order. While heroics were not desired, we decided that day against doing so—mainly because we had not fully given up on the idea that Joan might have more time and because of my belief that a DNR communicates to some medical personnel that a less urgent level of care is needed. Ten days later we would add the DNR.

Knowing that Johanna would be visiting Joan, one of the night nurses brought two bunnies to Joan's room. While this was against hospital policy, no one seemed to mind that she was sneaking new life onto a cancer floor. It was great fun. We all enjoyed holding them and letting them hop around on the bed. (Cleanup was not as much fun.)

During this week, Joan videotaped messages to our kids, Cathy, and me. Joan was frustrated because she had found it so difficult to write letters to the kids. Johanna had expressed that she would like some letters in case Joan would not be present at major life events. I suggested considering videotaping what she wanted to say. Joan's face lit up.

We asked Jonathan Ball, a friend and skilled social worker, if he would conduct the interview. He was pleased to do this. A few days later he videotaped Joan's twenty-five-minute message to our children. I asked Jonathan how it went. "Almost nothing to it. I just started the camera, and Joan did everything else. I didn't have to ask a question. It was extraordinary." I thought Jonathan was being modest and also perhaps overstating Joan's performance. Not so. Two evenings later, after Jonathan had completed taping Joan's messages to Cathy and me, Joan asked if I would watch the tape and give her feedback about whether it was okay. I was amazed at how clearly Joan articulated her love for each of us, and her thoughts and concerns. I remain awed by how focused and centered her messages are and by her capacity to convey her love, her appreciation, and her guidance. These messages are each an ongoing source of strength and a reminder of what an amazing woman I was fortunate to marry.

Farewell Messages

Part of what she said to me, Cathy, and the kids follows.

[Eric] You'll feel me. I know you are going to feel me in the Adirondacks. And I know I am not leaving you. We have talked about that many, many times. And your spirituality gives me strength because I know that you know—on a really important and on a real, honest level—that I am not leaving you at all, not one little bit in terms of my spirit. That I am much more than this. That I know that you believe that on a plane that even our kids can't get to and maybe shouldn't be able to get to yet. I am sorry that I can't, I can't make that journey together, or whatever.... I just don't think that anybody has quite that privilege to do it together. And I am sorry that there are going to be really grief-stricken, lonely times. But I don't think I am going to be feeling them, so I think you can take great—I hope, I really hope you can take satisfaction—I know you have said many times you want me "in the flesh", and, of course, in some respects I'd rather be in the flesh. But I am also so ready to be released. And I really hope you can get to the joy of that feeling of being released for me. I know you respect me, and that feels wonderful. And you have all of my respect. And, umm, I just want you to know how much I love you.

And I don't know if I'll miss you or not because I don't know exactly where I'll be. I feel like I am going to be in many ways having the easier job. And I am going to be there. I am there, and if anybody in the world that I know will be listening, it's going to be you. I know you are going to have your ears wide open. You're so receptive and you're so intuitive and you're so spiritual ... that even though I grieve for the grief you feel, I'll feel like it's cleansing. And I want you to feel my release as much as you can, even though it will be hard for you. . . . And I love you, you know that. I don't think I need to tell you I love you, but I will tell you anyway.

To Cathy she said,

It's just critical to me that you know from the bottom of my heart that you are the most precious, one of the most precious people in my life to me. That we will go on, that I know we will go on because I know . . . you have a deep spiritual sense of connection. And you'll be listening and I'll be there. And I think in many respects, more than anyone, you will have an appreciation of my release and a deep sense of relief for me. Because I know how wonderfully hard you have worked to protect me from those things that I don't want—like sometimes more pain or intervention or more western medicine, we call it. And I know that it has been very hard for Eric, being Eric, to accept me out of the flesh. And you have walked that very tight and balanced and difficult line in both supporting and understanding him—and really working to understand him and supporting and understanding my needs. . . . Anyway, I love you dearly. I'm there. And I think you know I'm there. And in our walks together, which will continue, I will be there and I know you will be open. I love you. You are just very precious. Thank you, Cathy.

And to the kids she ended her message:

I just adore you both. You taught me a lot. And I don't go in as much sadness as I go with a real feeling that, you know, that same feeling that I keep telling you. I am going to be there building those campfires for every one of you. Yours are going to be kind of last because you're coming last. But, anyway, I will be here and you know that. I am with you in every way but this bag of bones and blood and whatever—and that doesn't mean that much to me anymore—it's really, my spirit will be where you are. And I believe so much in you kids and am so proud of you, so very proud of you.

And go for walks, go for lots of walks and see me. I'll be there. No doubt I will be on your walks. That's going to be your closest place to get me. Be open to listening for me. Okay? Be open to my presence. Because I could be that deer swimming across the lake and if you are not open, you might miss me. But I think you will be open. Love you both. . . .

Final Days

I recall the remaining days as peaceful and immensely sad. Often with [friends and family] Cathy, Linda, and Michele, Joan would sit quietly, engaging in close conversation, punctuated by laughter and tears. Linda, a registered nurse, took over some of the care. Her exceptional wit was a welcomed distraction.

Around this time there were many other good-byes, in person and by telephone . . .

On May 7 Joan talked with Dr. Scalzo about hastening her death by stopping all hydration and nutrition. She was at peace knowing that she would be allowed to drift into a coma and be kept relatively pain free as she moved toward death. Dr. Richard Cheney stopped by at some point, the doctor who had done his best to get Joan on C-225 [a drug that slows cancer growth]. Joan had previously complimented his choice of a tie, showing a dolphin jumping out of the ocean. He leaned over and presented the tie to her as a gift.

Joan put a call in to Nancy Kemeny. We long since learned that Dr. Kemeny, who first struck us as cold, was deeply caring of her patients. And the three of us had developed a close cooperative relationship. Joan expressed her appreciation to Dr. Kemeny. Both cried.

The Hardest Goodbyes

The hardest good-byes were with Aaron and Johanna. I do not know what words passed as each sat for final discussions with Joan, but I know Joan felt gratified by the love and closeness she felt with each. She was concerned with how the children would handle the loss but optimistic about the children she had raised and their capacity to live good, happy, and kind lives . . .

I recall how in October 1998, as we drove to Sloan, Joan burst out crying as we listened to music from *Les Misérables*, the song in which Cosette's dying mother entrusts her upbringing to Jean Valjean. Joan, who had lost her mother when she was six, could not fathom leaving Johanna or Aaron without a mother. Now the time had come to take leave.

Earlier in this thirty-two-month marathon, Gussie Sorenson, the social worker at Hematology-Oncology, commented that "as you go along this journey, you may find that you redefine what you mean by 'hope.'" Yes, Gussie was right. Where once we had hoped for a reprieve, then a cure, and then some quality time, now Joan hoped for gentle release. And I turned my hope to there being more to life and love than what is visibly present.

Mary Jo, Cathy, Linda, and Michele were all present during the last few days and, of course, Aaron and Johanna. As Joan drifted in and out of consciousness, she spoke of feeling her mother's presence, of feeling she was going home. We began making preparations for the funeral, identifying a cemetery, and asking Terry Culbertson if she would officiate.

The hospital staff were exceptionally kind and concerned. A pain-free death was now the goal, the hope. During the final nights, I often stood by her bed and held her hand, telling her how much I loved her and coaching, "It's okay, Hon, it's time to let go. It's time to die."

On May 10, Mary Jo and Linda stayed overnight in the room with Joan and me. At the slightest sign of discomfort, we would request more morphine for Joan. The next day, Joan's last, was peaceful. That night I slept sitting up in a chair next to her, my left hand on her chest, my head by her side and my right hand on her head. I would wake and ask Reeja

Luthra, the night nurse we had gotten to know, to give Joan more medication to make her more comfortable. She did. In the morning I woke to Reeja standing over Joan, still warm. "Is she gone?" I asked. Reeja checked Joan's heartbeat. Joan had been released. She was at peace and the room felt peaceful. But how missed she was and still is.

Making the Most of the Time I Have Left

Laurence Shames and Peter Barton

Peter Barton led an extraordinarily successful life. A pioneer in the cable television industry (he also helped co-found MTV), Barton stood at the top of his career while still a relatively young man. Barton's life was not all about material success, though—he always tried to enjoy all aspects of life, from working as a professional freestyle skier to becoming active in politics.

Considering Barton's "no-holds-barred" approach to life, it's no surprise that when he was diagnosed with a rare, inoperable form of stomach cancer in 1997, he threw himself just as wholeheartedly into a variety of new pursuits. These included teaching and founding nonprofit organizations, but also—and most importantly to Barton—focusing on his family. In this essay, Barton describes how his terminal cancer diagnosis dramatically changed his approach to his kids' education.

Peter Barton died in September 2002.

Sometime around the end of 1996, I threw myself a party.

It was a very odd sort of party, in that it didn't happen at any particular place or time, and no one but Laura and I realized it was happening at all. But it was a celebration nonetheless, complete with champagne, and a giddy break from the usual routines, and even the counter-current of melancholy that often goes with parties.

The occasion was not a birthday or an anniversary. It was the fact that I had now outlived my father.

This was a huge milestone for me, as well as a genuine surprise. I was forty-five and a half years old and my heart hadn't yet given out. All those hours on the treadmill, all those years of saying no to the butter and the Brie had paid off.

Having expected a radically short life, and having pushed myself accordingly, I now felt like a gambler playing with house money. No matter what bet I made next, I was ahead of the game. I'd *won*. I could elbow in at any table. There was a freedom and a gratitude in this that almost made me dizzy. I was determined to make the most of it.

Time to Move On

On April Fools' Day of 1997, at a breakfast meeting with John Malone, I resigned as president of Liberty. I was a few days shy of my forty-sixth birthday.

From everyone's perspective but my own, this decision seemed wildly abrupt and unexpected. But in fact it was part of a long-considered plan. It was never my intention to keep that—or any—job forever. I only like a job when I'm still learning, when I really don't know what I'm doing, when I can feel the thrill of performing without a safety net. After six years at Liberty, I was doing things by rote. Why? To make more money I didn't really need or even want? To prove to myself that I was still a player?

The reasons to continue seemed woefully inadequate. And truthfully, the cable industry was not nearly as much fun as it had once been. Success had made it dull. Its vast size had rendered it conservative. Inevitably, huge and sluggish organizations now controlled it.

New Adventures, Exciting Possibilities

Besides, I was ready for a new adventure. You could call it a midlife crisis—except that I was way past midlife, and besides, I had a "crisis" every decade or so. Now, again, I felt a hankering for one of those extreme and exhilarating direction changes that have defined my path and kept me juiced.

My possibilities were nothing short of mouthwatering. False modesty aside, now that I was in my prime I had the resources and the connections so that whatever I did I could reasonably expect to do it at the highest level.

From my days in state government I had retained an unwavering belief in the value of public service. Now, because of relationships I'd forged within the Democratic Party, I had reason to hope that I might at some point be tapped for an ambassadorship.

I still loved media, and thought my knowledge of that field might be helpful in the nonprofit arena. I explored the notion of running National Public Radio.

The entrepreneurial side of business still excited me, and the Internet, in 1997, looked more than a little like cable TV had looked in 1982. I spoke with the boards of Yahoo, AOL, and Microsoft about creating a billion-dollar incubator for promising e-commerce companies.

Lacking Confidence

Yes, I was thinking big. And loving it. My life was still tracing out my generation's happy arc. Next stop: elder statesman.

But here's something that's slightly embarrassing to admit. I've acknowledged before that true confidence did not come naturally to me; insecurity has been a constant companion and a constant goad. And in 1997, even as I was fantasizing a great next phase, I was secretly afraid that, without my job title, I would quickly be forgotten, pushed aside. Peter who? What's he done lately? I honestly worried that people would no longer take my calls.

Maybe I'm paranoid. Or maybe the business world really is that fickle. Either way, the fear was real enough. And now that I think of it, maybe that's partly why the writing of this book has become so important to me. It would be comforting to feel I've done something that can't be so easily erased.

A Different Dilemma

In any event, the dilemma of my next big plan soon became moot. Blindsided by cancer, I watched my grand schemes go out the window. Yearning for health, working for survival, became my major occupation.

I'm wistful, of course, about the things I might have accomplished and didn't. Success—make no mistake—is the ultimate baby boomer drug, and, in my middle forties, I craved another dose. But if illness put the kibosh on my exploits in the wider world, there was a compensating good that came of this: it focused my attention on things closer to home, on more intimate arenas where, I hoped, I could still make a difference.

A Choice to Make a Difference

So, for instance, I volunteered to teach a class in the business school of the University of Denver. I wanted to preach the gospel of entrepreneurship. I wanted at least some small number of MBAs to understand that their real mission lay far beyond mere number crunching or consulting.

I started the Privacy Foundation, a nonprofit resource dedicated to helping people protect themselves from unwarranted snooping, especially through the Internet, by government, and commercial interests.

But the thing I feel best about is that, freed from the demands of conventional "work," I had the great privilege of getting involved, in a really hands-on way, in my kids' education.

I'm not talking about the schoolroom here. I'm talking about exposure to the real world.

One day my kids had some friends over. I eavesdropped as they were having the what-does-your-dad-do conversation. When it was Jeff and Chris's turn to talk, they couldn't quite explain what my job had been. They knew it had to do with television, that I used to fly to meetings. Beyond that, they really didn't have a clue.

It's not that I hadn't told them. It's that what I did was too abstract. There was nothing you could hold in your hand for show-and-tell.

All the kids agreed on which dad had the coolest job: a guy who made screen doors. *That* was something a son or daughter could point to with pride.

What Kids Need

I learned something from that conversation. Kids—both boys and girls—need nuts and bolts. Screwdrivers and lathes. To feel at ease in the world, they have to learn what the world is actually made of, and how it got that way.

Just as it's crucial for underprivileged kids to be shown that there are possibilities beyond their neighborhoods, it's also important for overprivileged kids to see other sides of life.

I didn't want my kids to grow up in an abstract world of deals and numbers and money that just happened. I wanted them to understand that people worked hard, at a gloriously wide range of things, and that there was dignity in all of them.

So I bought a big stretch van—my rolling locker room—and started taking my kids and their friends on what I thought of as Real World Outings. They were like school field trips, but without the onus of school. I was never "Mr. Barton." I was always Peter. I wanted the kids to be able to relax, to let off steam. If things got too rambunctious in the back of the van, I'd yell out, "Hey, what's rule number one?"

The kids would scream back, "No permanent injuries!"

And they'd settle down—a little. I loved it.

A Rolling Classroom

Every outing had a theme. "Grease"—where we looked closely at the realities of fast food. "Garbage"—where we followed the trail of household trash, and of recycled cars and asphalt and concrete.

One of my favorites was called "Luggage." There's a Samsonite factory in Denver; we went to it and saw the bags being made, heard the honest clank of rivets. Then we went to a retail store and asked a lot of questions: Who decided how things would be displayed? How did you figure out how many to keep in the warehouse? Who bought more luggage—men or women?

Then we drove out to the airport, having gotten permission to go "backstage" with the baggage handlers. We watched them, with their back-support belts and their elastic wristbands and their boots. Bend and jerk; bend and jerk. We saw how many suitcases they lifted, how heavy the bags were, how they just kept coming down the conveyor, relentless. . . .

Sometimes, at the end of our outings, there'd be the strangest sound in the van: silence. How rare was that? Ten or twelve kids, thinking something over.

A Smaller-Scale Adventure

By the time I was leading these forays, death was growing inside me. I'd outlived my father, but, by some perverse logic, that very milestone seemed to mark the beginning of my own decline. My future ended almost as soon as it started.

Still, I was thoroughly enjoying this next adventure. It was an adventure on a beautifully intimate scale. If I still had the strength and luck to accomplish anything at this stage, it wouldn't be reported in *Who's Who* or the *Wall Street Journal*. But maybe it would be scrawled here and there in a child's notebook, or etched into a young and open mind.

I could think of no better way to use the time that remained for me.

Learning to Talk about Dying

Jerome Groopman

One of the most delicate and difficult aspects of practicing oncology is working with dying patients and their families. As Dr. Jerome Groopman notes, few oncologists feel comfortable talking with cancer sufferers about end-of-life issues, and medical students receive almost no training in discussing death and dying with their patients and their loved ones.

Dr. Groopman's experiences—and mistakes—as a young medical intern, as well as the traumatic event of witnessing his own father's death, encouraged him to find honest, compassionate ways to discuss death with his terminally ill patients. Using the example of one young breast cancer patient, Dr. Groopman illustrates how truthful, open communication can ease patients' suffering and allow them to face death with understanding and dignity.

Dr. Jerome Groopman, a faculty member at Harvard Medical School, received his medical degree from Columbia and practices oncology in the Boston area. In addition to conducting research on both cancer and AIDS, Dr. Groopman also provides public education on these health issues and writes about the spiritual dimensions of health care and illness in books such as The Anatomy of Hope *and* The Measure of Our Days.

Not long ago, I had an appointment with a patient who was likely to die within a year and a half. Maxine Barlow was a twenty-eight-year-old teacher in Boston. The only child of a middle-class family, she had recently become engaged to a financial analyst, Peter Wayland (all names have been changed). One morning in the shower, Maxine found a small lump in her breast, a little larger than a pea. A biopsy showed that it was breast cancer. Further tests revealed that the cancer had spread to Maxine's spine and liver, which meant that surgery could not fully remove it, and Maxine's surgeon referred her to me for chemotherapy.

Maxine and I met on a brisk autumn afternoon. Her appointment was my last of the day, since our conversation was likely to extend beyond the hour usually allotted to new patients. I had to explain the gravity of her condition and the possible choices she could make.

After I had examined Maxine, we were joined in my office by her parents and by Peter. They sat in a semicircle facing me, with Maxine between them. I moved my chair out from behind my desk.

"Let's review what was found at surgery," I began. Maxine reached for Peter's hand. Although I addressed Maxine, I also briefly met the gaze of her parents and of Peter, in order to engage everyone. "The cancer in the breast measured one and a half centimeters, about half an inch, and under the microscope the cancer cells were actively dividing," I said. "They should be treated aggressively. The tests we did on the tumor showed that it is not sensitive to hormones"—which ruled out Tamoxifen, a common hormone-blocker. "The scan showed that several deposits of tumor had spread from the breast to the bones in the neck. There also are four deposits in the liver. We can treat them with chemotherapy, which destroys the cancer cells wherever they might be lurking. The good news is that you stand a very strong chance of going into remission."

The Meaning of Remission

"So that means that she'll be O.K.?" Maxine's mother asked.

My stomach tightened in a familiar way. This part never got any easier.

"Remission does not mean cure," I said. "Remission means that all the cancer we can measure disappears. Therapy is palliative [controlling, not curing, symptoms]."

"What do you mean, 'palliative'?" Peter asked in a panicked voice.

"She has to be cured," Maxine's father said.

This distinction was important, and I needed to make sure, gently but unequivocally, that they understood. "There is a very good chance that we will see the metastatic deposits in your bones and liver shrink significantly, or completely melt away. But the most intensive chemotherapy or radiation available—even bone-marrow transplant—is not enough to destroy every cancer cell in your body. That is why, currently, we cannot say the cancer can be cured."

Maxine sat without speaking. Her eyes filled with tears, and I gave her some tissues.

"What is the point of treatment, then?" I asked. "Palliation. That means that even if the cancer cannot be cured it can be controlled. The best-case scenario is that the cancer becomes like a parasite," I said, purposefully invoking a stark image. "We knock it down with the therapy, and hope that it stays down for many, many months or years. You can live an active life—work, jog, travel, whatever. The bones and liver can heal. And when the cancer returns we work to knock it down again. All the while, we hold on to the hope that an experimental treatment will be found that is able to eradicate the cancer—to truly cure you."

The Worst-Case Scenario

Like Maxine, Mrs. Barlow was fighting back tears. Her husband stared at me. I paused before broaching a second critical issue.

"We talked about the best-case scenario. But we also have to acknowledge that there is a worst-case scenario." I had found that this part of the discussion was best completed rapidly, as if removing an adhesive bandage.

"The worst-case scenario is that ultimately the cancer becomes resistant to all the treatments we have, and even experimental therapies are no use. Most people say that if they reach a point in the illness when their brain is impaired, and there is no likelihood of improving their quality of life, then nothing should be done to keep them artificially alive, through machines like respirators. It's essential, Maxine, that I know what you want done if we reach that point."

"I—I don't think I would want that," she said, haltingly.

"You mean that you would want only comfort measures to alleviate pain, and nothing done to prolong your life, like a respirator or cardiac resuscitation?"

"Yes, I think so," Maxine whispered.

I nodded. This was her "end-of-life directive." I would put it in writing in her medical chart.

"We have a plan of therapy and an understanding. Now let's look on the positive side," I said, trying to spark some of the determination she would need in order to endure the months of chemotherapy ahead. "You are young, your organ function is excellent—despite the deposits of tumor, your liver is still working well, and your blood counts are fine—so there is every reason to think that you will tolerate the drugs and we will make real progress."

I smiled confidently. Maxine struggled to do the same.

"But what are the exact odds for a remission?" Peter Wayland asked. "I mean, how many patients like Maxie stay in remission and for how long, on average?"

Maxine looked at him sharply. "Dr. Groopman said that there is every reason to think I'll go into remission," she said. "What more do we need to know now?"

She turned to me, her face full of uncertainty.

Softening the Statistics

This was a crucial moment in our interview. There were several ways that I could answer Peter's question. I could give the bald statistics—that more than fifty per cent of people with cancer like Maxine's die within two years—or I could put it more gently, and say that she had a chance, if a low one, of surviving for more than two years. I could even say, somewhat vaguely, that she was young and strong and had as good a chance as anyone of surviving, on the principle that she would benefit more from encouragement than from statistics. As I looked at Maxine, I sensed that she preferred neither the extreme of ignorance nor the extreme of excruciating detail but some middle ground.

"Statistics don't say anything about any particular individual, only about groups," I said. "There can be wide variability in the behavior of any cancer in each person, because each of us is different—different genetically, living in a different environment—and we metabolize the treatments differently.

"I want my patients to be informed," I said, looking now at Peter. "When Maxine said she understood there is a very good chance of remission, that is accurate. It could last months or it could last years. Putting precise numbers on it at this point doesn't really tell us anything more about Maxine. In the meantime, we need to plan for the best while acknowledging the worst."

Giving Bad News

Oncologists give bad news to patients some thirty-five times per month on average, telling a patient that he has cancer, that his tumor has come back, that his treatment has failed, that no further treatment would be helpful. And yet there is no agreement among specialists about how to deliver such news. More than forty percent of oncologists withhold a prognosis from a patient if he or she does not ask for it or if the family requests that the patient not be told. A similar number speak in euphemisms, skirting the truth. Today [2002], in most of Europe, doctors often do not tell patients that they are dying. . . .

As medical practice grows more sophisticated more people are living longer with the knowledge that they may be dying.

Decisions made in the late stages of illness are increasingly an aspect of treatment. Dying requires emotional and physical stamina from the individual and his family. And the difficulty of negotiating all this has an effect on doctors as well as patients. A recent article reported that more than half of the oncologists interviewed say that the frequent witnessing of death leads to an overwhelming sense of fatigue and futility; the profession has one of the highest burnout rates in medicine.

Despite this, during my nine years of medical school and professional training in the nineteen-seventies, I was never instructed in how to speak about dying to a gravely ill patient and the patient's family. It was presumed that, as medical students, we learned how to deliver bad news through careful observation of our mentors, just as we learned how to lance a deep abscess by watching doctors and then trying it ourselves. But most physicians preferred to speak to their patients in private. And the subject was never raised in our classrooms.

I Learned from Past Mistakes

As an oncology fellow, I began my career believing that it was essential to provide details to my patients. Sharing statistics seemed like the obvious thing to do: surely a patient should have access to everything I knew. Early on, I had a case somewhat similar to Maxine's. Claire Allen was a small, straw-haired librarian in her forties with breast cancer; she was married, with two young children. Like Maxine, she had multiple metastases to bone and liver. We met in my clinic office, and she looked at me expectantly.

"Claire, with this disease, a remission would ordinarily last three to six months," I told her bluntly. "A person could expect to survive between one to two years."

She appeared to take the news stalwartly, but I later learned from her husband that she had left the appointment deeply shaken. She told her children that she had only one Christmas left. Her face was full of despair whenever I saw her. And yet

Claire lived for nearly four years. She was able to travel, work part time, and take care of her children, but was unable to stop thinking that she could die at any moment.

Chastened, I tried a different approach. Henry Gold, a short-order cook in his sixties, had acute leukemia that had resisted all treatment. At one point, he asked me what else could be done. I reassured him that there were drugs that had not yet been tried, even though I knew they were unlikely to help. When Henry started to bleed around his lungs, I had the interns drain the hemorrhage with chest tubes; I insisted that he be intubated [a tube inserted to ventilate lungs], supported on a respirator in the I.C.U., and given numerous blood transfusions. His heart developed a dangerous arrhythmia, so I gave orders for cardiac medications and electroshock. I never asked Henry what he wanted. He stayed alive for more than a week on the respirator, a catheter in his heart, tubes in his throat, unable to speak to family and friends who had come to his bedside.

The First Round of Chemotherapy

On a chilly morning two days after our first meeting, Maxine returned to the clinic for her first round of chemotherapy. She had insisted on coming alone; Peter would pick her up afterward. The chemotherapy suite is a large, open space that holds twenty or so patients receiving intravenous drugs, some behind curtains, others talking or watching television. Maxine looked at the patients she passed.

Most were wearing hats or kerchiefs to cover their bald heads. Several reclined in their chairs, thin and pale, too weak to sit up. It was clear that some of them would soon die.

A half hour after Maxine's chemotherapy treatment, Peter still had not arrived. Maxine's cell phone rang. "He's tied up," she explained to me, and we arranged for a car service to take her home. When I called Maxine later that evening to see how she was doing, Peter answered the phone and told me that she was sleeping.

"She's going to die, isn't she?" he said. He explained that he had been searching the Internet, and had read that in cases like Maxine's patients survived on average eighteen months, and that a remission lasted three to six months at best.

"Peter, as I said when we met, statistics don't tell you what is going to happen to any one person, just groups."

I got off the phone as quickly as I could. There could be no "back channel" discussions with friends or family; if Maxine had wanted to, she could have logged on to the Internet.

A Disturbing New Development

Over the next seven months, the metastases in Maxine's bones and in her liver decreased significantly. Although she was frequently tired and lost her hair, she was able to work part time, and even took a weekend trip to Manhattan with her parents and went to Newport for a friend's wedding. Then, on a routine visit at the end of May, after her eighth month of therapy, I noticed that one of her eyes wandered, and she seemed to be tilting her head to the right.

"Are you having any trouble seeing?"

She said that sometimes it was difficult to read.

"Any double vision?"

Yes, she said, on a few occasions that week, when she was walking down stairs.

Movement of the eyes is controlled by a set of cranial nerves at the base of the skull. An initial MRI [magnetic resonance imaging] scan of the brain did not turn up anything abnormal, but scans do not always detect small deposits on the cranial nerves. I explained that a spinal tap was the best way to determine if the cancer had spread to the brain; it would allow us to search for tumor cells in the spinal fluid.

Maxine lay on her side as a medical resident performed the procedure. I tried to distract her. We talked about the Red Sox, who had started the season strong, and whether, as usual, they would end up losing games in the homestretch. After sterilizing and anesthetizing the area between the fourth and fifth lumbar vertebrae, the resident passed a fine trocar [a sharp instrument used as a drainage outlet] into the spinal canal. Maxine twitched. Drops of fluid fell from the trocar into a test tube that he held under it. Normal spinal fluid is clear; Maxine's was cloudy.

A Major Setback

"It's over," I said. "Stay down for an hour, so you don't get a headache."

She asked what it meant if the cancer had gone to her cranial nerves.

I was almost certain, based on the cloudiness of the spinal fluid, that this was the case. How much did Maxine want to know?

"It is a major setback," I said.

"I'm not sure I want to ask how long a remission lasts if the cancer is in my brain," she said.

"Are you sure you want to talk about this now?"

Maxine closed her eyes and nodded.

"People usually live several weeks to a few months without any treatment," I said. "But that represents the average. There are people who live longer. Treatment with radiation and chemotherapy instilled into the spinal fluid may or may not extend life, but it can reduce some of the most annoying complications, like the double vision."

Maxine was silent. "Is it even worth being treated?" she finally asked.

"You are the only one who can answer that question," I said. "If we don't treat it, it will quickly spread to other cranial nerves and parts of the brain and spinal cord. The quality of your life would be markedly impaired. I want to help sustain as much quality of life for as long as possible."

Maxine opened her eyes.

"I don't want to die," she said, beginning to sob. "I didn't think it would happen so fast, so soon. I'm not ready to die."

"I don't want to lose you," I said. There was nothing more I could say now that would help. "Let's go step by step, and talk after the results from the spinal tap."

Speaking Frankly

Later that day, I went to the pathology laboratory. Under the microscope, numerous large cells, with distorted nuclei, filled what should have been an empty field. "Carcinoma," the pathologist said.

Over the next few weeks, we began radiation treatment and a new round of chemotherapy, infused into her spinal fluid. At first, Maxine's double vision improved. But after three weeks or so she found that she couldn't move her left eye, and we put a patch over it. Shortly thereafter, the left side of her face began to droop. A second MRI showed that the cancer had spread to the membranes lining the cerebral cortex and spinal cord. It was evening when I came into Maxine's hospital room. She was watching television. . . .

"I'm not sure how much strength I have left," Maxine said. She was in a fragile condition. It was time to assess clinical issues.

"Remember once I asked you what your wishes were if we reached a point when further therapy would not improve the quality of your life?"

Maxine nodded. "So you think it's just a few days?" she asked. Her voice was hollow.

"Probably more than just a few days," I said. "Probably weeks. Or maybe longer—I've been wrong before."

"And really nothing can be done?"

Like all patients, Maxine was finding it almost impossible to give up hope.

"Nothing that I know of," I said. "And to continue to give you chemotherapy would not improve the time we have left. But anything I can do to make the time that we have left good for you, I'll do."

Maxine turned away. "How do I actually die from the cancer?"

"You lose consciousness, go into a coma, and either you stop breathing or your heart stops. But you're not aware of any of it."

She was silent as I sat holding her hand.

A Personal Recollection

The first time I witnessed death was in my second year of medical school. My father had had a massive, unexpected heart attack, and I went to meet my mother at the hospital in Queens. The sheets were drenched with sweat. His eyes were filmy and repeatedly rolled upward. Coarse, grunting noises punctuated his breathing, and his chest heaved. His limbs jerked wildly. This went on for nearly half an hour, as a large clock on the wall ticked off the minutes. Then, after a last convulsion, a pink foam poured from his mouth, his head snapped back, the little color remaining in his skin drained away, and he was still.

I held my mother, numb with disbelief. The doctor on call, whom we did not know and who had stood by as we watched, closed the curtain around the bed. He looked at me holding my mother, and said weakly, "It's tough, kid."

Although I later learned that the flailing movements of my father's limbs were the result of neurological reflexes, and that he had not been conscious, I could not stop wondering if he had suffered. The ugliness of these final minutes often invades otherwise comforting memories of times we spent together. When I became a physician, I vowed that I would do everything I could to temper such gruesome experiences for the patient and for the family....

Preparing for the End

After I talked with Maxine, I arranged for her to be transferred to a special hospice unit [a facility for caring for the terminally ill], and soon she began to drift in and out of consciousness. The cancer pressing on the cranial nerves connected to the back of her throat and her tongue had made it difficult for her to swallow. The nurses had to suction her saliva to prevent her from choking. Shortly before noon a week later, I was paged and told that Maxine's death appeared imminent.

Maxine's parents were sitting by her bed when I came in. They stood up, and Mrs. Barlow hugged me, crying. Mr. Barlow's face was frozen with grief.

Maxine was no longer conscious. Every few seconds, her chest heaved, and she gasped. She was entering what is called the agonal phase—taken from the Greek *agon*, which means struggle—a period that precedes death and can last from a few minutes to hours.

I warned Maxine's parents that this was usually harrowing, and that sometimes family members preferred not to witness it.

"I want to be with my baby," Maxine's mother said.

Maxine's hands began to twitch and her breathing moved into a syncopated pattern called Cheyne-Stokes, a short set of staccato breaths bracketing a long pause.

Mrs. Barlow raised her head.

"Maxie, we love you, and God loves you."

Mr. Barlow sat straight, his hands clasped in his lap.

Sometimes as a patient dies there is a convulsive burst of muscular activity, like a grand-mal seizure. I braced myself for it when Maxine's fingers began to twitch, as if she were grasping for an invisible object. These muscle contractions continued for some forty minutes. Then a harsh rattling sound came from her chest. I glanced at the nurse, who was next to the morphine infusion. There was a single explosive jerk of

Maxine's body, a sharp arching of her chest, followed by a series of fluttering movements in the muscles of her neck.

The Barlows stood up. Maxine's skin was already changing to an ashen hue. I placed my stethoscope over her heart. "I am sorry," the nurse said. I reached over and took Mr. Barlow's hand, and then turned and embraced Mrs. Barlow as she cried. I left the Barlows and went to the nurses' station to fill out Maxine's death certificate. I designated the primary cause as respiratory failure due to metastatic breast cancer to the brain and handed the chart with the death certificate to the floor clerk. The time of death was 12:57 P.M.

Losing a Child

Maria Housden

Maria Housden's daughter Hannah was diagnosed with termi-
nal stomach cancer one month before her third birthday. Here
Housden gives readers a glimpse into Hannah's final weeks, illus-
trating the fearless, almost joyful attitude Housden's young
daughter possessed about her own illness and death.

In these passages, Housden illustrates the importance of
speaking candidly with ill children and their siblings about
death. She also describes how Hannah's matter-of-fact approach
influenced her mother's attitude toward life and faith. Although
Housden is grieving the imminent loss of her daughter, she finds
strength and wisdom in the most unexpected place—in the
simple words and brave example of three-year-old Hannah.

Hannah died in 1994. Maria Housden's memoir about her
young daughter's illness and death is titled Hannah's Gift: Lessons from a Life Fully Lived.

I was sitting in a rocking chair in our bedroom, nursing
Margaret, who was a week old. Will was sitting on the floor,
staring out the window. A picture book about dinosaurs lay
open at his feet. Hannah was on the bed, lying in a half-seated
position against a pile of pillows, covered by her pink blanket.
Her eyes were closed, but I didn't think she was asleep.

Several days before, she had announced, "I hurt too much.
I want to sleep in the bed that smells like you and Daddy."

Her tumor was growing rapidly now, large enough to press
against her ribs and spinal cord. Although a constant dose of
morphine was being pumped into her body, twenty-four hours

a day, Hannah could no longer walk; she had to be carried. Other than asking to go to the toilet, she seemed content to stay where she was.

Where Are the Experts?

I felt frustrated that there wasn't more I could do to help Hannah, and longed for information about how to prepare her and us for her death. Pat had given me what she could, but the hospice [a facility for caring for the terminally ill]she worked for rarely dealt with dying children; none of the hospices in our area did. It seemed almost inconceivable to me that there had been shelves of books, videos, and even classes at the hospital to prepare Hannah for Margaret's birth. Where were the experts now, when I needed to prepare her for her death?

I had done my best to anticipate what Hannah might need. The antique rocking chair was a testament to that. It had always been Hannah's favorite spot to snuggle and read. I had asked Claude to bring it upstairs, imagining it would be the perfect place for us to spend her final days. I was wrong. "It hurts too much," she said. My image of us rocking peacefully into her death was simply one more thing I had to let go of.

Hard Questions

Will looked up.

"Mom, how long does it take a body to become a skeleton?"

Hannah heard Will's question. Her eyes popped open. These days, death was one of her favorite subjects.

You've got to be kidding, I thought. I was all for telling the truth and facing fears; but I wasn't ready for *this* conversation.

"I'm not sure, Will," I said, feeling that I didn't want to know, either.

He screwed up his lips and creased his brow, as if he were contemplating probable rates of decomposition. Hannah had her own ideas.

"You know," she said, her eyes bright with mischief, "they can bury your body, but they can't bury your spirit!"

She was grinning. Will looked at her and grinned, too.

"That's great, Hannah," he said. He turned to me.

"What do you think, Mom? Do our spirits go to heaven even though our bodies are buried?"

I had been waiting for this question for a while. I had even wondered if I should bring it up myself. I loved that the two of them had done it on their own.

"Well," I began, my thoughts tripping seven sentences ahead of my words, "I believe that when the body is too sick or too old to live anymore, it dies, and then the soul is free."

No Easy Answers

"What happens to the soul after the body dies, Mom?" Will asked.

"I'm not really sure," I admitted. "Some people believe that souls go to heaven after the body dies. I think I believe that, too."

"Me, too," said Hannah.

Will wanted to know more. "I know the Bible says that, but does anybody else?" he asked.

"Well," I answered, "I've been reading books about something called a 'near-death experience.' Sometimes people die for a few minutes, like in very serious surgeries or car accidents, but then doctors manage to bring them back to life. When this happens, those people describe death as a long tunnel with a bright light at the other end that draws them into a place of beautiful love. Not everyone believes that's what happens. I guess we can't be sure until we do it ourselves."

I continued. "You know how a butterfly grows inside the cocoon until it's ready to fly? Or the way a hermit crab lives in a shell until it gets too small for his growing body and then moves to another? I like to think death is something like that."

97

"I'm going to be a butterfly," Hannah stated, and with that settled, rolled back onto the pillows and shut her eyes.

Indulging in Fantasies

Hannah was dozing on one side of the bed, her long legs barely covered by her pink blanket. She was wearing only a pair of cotton underpants.

"Clothes are too scratchy," she had said.

One of her arms lay across Margaret, who was asleep next to her, tightly bundled in fuzzy pink pajamas. The hum of the air conditioner in the window accounted for the nip in the air despite the fact that the late July sun was baking the roof overhead. The sicker Hannah got, the colder she wanted the room to be.

I rocked to the rhythm of the morphine pump's click. As Hannah's tumor grew, so did the amount of morphine she required. I was grateful for the way the drug seemed to dull Hannah's pain, but the more effective it was, the easier it was to deny that she was sick enough to die. For days now, I had fantasized that she might wake up, ask to get dressed, and suggest we all go out to dinner. Claude seemed even more lost in the fantasy. Every time Dr. Kamalaker had prescribed an increase in her dose, he questioned the need to do it, explaining that he was afraid she might get addicted. Nobody had the heart to tell him that addiction is not possible for someone who is dead.

I continued to rock back and forth. A stack of books on the dresser with titles like *Living with Death and Dying*, *Embraced by the Light*, and *How to Go on Living When Someone You Love Dies* was as neglected as the shriveled piece of cheese that Hannah had requested and then refused to eat. Even her Christmas dress, which she had asked me to hang on the curtain rod where she could see it, seemed to be holding its breath.

Renewed Interest in Life

I closed my eyes. My lids felt heavy and warm from too little sleep. I could feel Hannah looking at me. I opened my eyes slowly. Her arms were outstretched, reaching for me.

"Mommy, I want you to carry me to my room."

I came alive. It was the first time in days she had asked to go anywhere other than the bathroom. Perhaps this was the moment everything had been waiting for. Hannah was taking an interest in life again. I gently and gingerly ran my hands under her bony hips and back and lifted her from the bed. I moved slowly to give her body time to adjust. I could almost hear her internal organs groan as the tumor shifted its bulk inside her. Hannah wrapped her thin arms around my neck and locked her legs around my hips. She pinned herself against me with a strength that surprised me. Her head rested on my shoulder. I breathed her in, felt her soft, "woolly mammoth" hair against my cheek. Her body was unnaturally warm given the coolness of the room. She was burning with a fever that would not break. Her chest rose and fell against mine, and I could feel both of our hearts beating—mine slow and deep, hers quick and light.

As I lifted her from the bed, I tried to imagine her sitting on the floor of her room, surrounded by baby dolls and dress-up clothes. I knew the image was as fragile as a painter's wet canvas. As I adjusted Hannah's position on my hip, she winced. The image slid out of my mind. I tried desperately not to jiggle or jar her too much as I carried her down the stairs. When we got to the doorway of her room, Hannah reached out and grabbed the wooden molding.

"Don't put me down and don't go in," she said. "I just want to look."

On the Threshold

The two of us stood on the threshold, watching dust dance in the late afternoon sun. A pink comforter and her cow-jumping-over-the-moon quilt stretched neatly, without wrinkles, across her bed. Dolls and stuffed animals stared blankly from their perches on the shelf. Two seashells from a preschool field trip leaned against each other on top of her dresser. The magic wand she had made at her birthday party almost a year ago lay in the middle of the floor. I wanted to wave it through the hush and bring everything back to life.

I knew she was saying good-bye, but I wasn't ready. This room with its sugar-pink sweetness, Barbie dolls, and red patent leather shoes *was* Hannah. If I were to say good-bye to this, what part of her would be left?

Releasing her grip on the door frame, Hannah wrapped her arms around my neck, and buried her face in my shoulder.

"I'm ready to go back now," she said.

As we climbed the stairs, I walked as slowly as I could, savoring the closeness of her. Before returning her to the nest of pillows and blankets, I stood silently, swaying from side to side, as if in a trance. I didn't want to let her go. I wanted to remain in this moment forever.

I thought about her room, how possible and yet inconceivable it was that she would never see it again. I wondered if it would always wait for her to return, if it would always be her room, if it would ever forget. I wondered the same things about myself: if I could accept that she would never return, if I would always feel like her mother, if I would ever forget.

Unwilling to Accept

I was sitting at the foot of the bed, snuggling Margaret. It was early in the day. Claude had left for work. Will was sitting on the floor, eating cereal and watching TV.

Hannah stirred and sat up slowly. I turned to look at her. Her skin was almost translucent. She hadn't eaten more than a bite or two of solid food for almost a week. As she had grown thinner, her tumor had grown bigger. Her left side was swollen grotesquely out of proportion. The skin that stretched across her ribs was deep purple from the mass of blood vessels that had accumulated there in a vain attempt to sate the cancer's appetite for blood. Sometimes she asked me to rub her side. I hated knowing that as I lovingly ran my cool palms over her hot, numb skin, I was gently caressing her tumor. Hannah had made friends with it somehow, treating it gingerly, deferentially, adjusting her pillows so it could rest on a cushion of softness. I wasn't willing. I wanted it to be gone.

Hannah looked at me. She winced, and then smiled.

A Leap of Faith

"Mommy," she said quietly, "do you know that even if I go to heaven, I'm going to come back?"

I paused before answering. I wanted to tell her the truth. The problem was, I wasn't sure exactly what the truth was. I had read that grieving children under the age of six imagine death as a short absence and expect loved ones to return sometime after the funeral. I wondered if this was what Hannah thought, too.

I took a breath. Hannah was grinning now, her head cocked to one side. I studied her face. She looked light, expectant, unconcerned. I felt as if she was reading my mind, and was amused by my dilemma. I closed my eyes for a moment. There, behind my eyelids, I saw something I could hardly believe: It was Hannah, dancing in the sparkly darkness, radiant, laughing, and waving. I grinned, my eyes still closed.

In that instant I knew that, no matter what happened, there was a part of Hannah that would always be with me, something of her that would never die. It wasn't a belief. It wasn't a hope. It was a knowing beyond the workings of my mind, the quietest, deepest experience of faith I had ever known.

I opened my eyes and let go of the breath I had been holding in my heart.

"Yes, Hannah, I know," I said.

Hannah leaned back into the pillows, closed her eyes, and smiled.

SOCIAL ISSUES
FIRSTHAND

CHAPTER 4

Surviving and Thriving

Cancer Didn't Make Me a Better Person

Suellen Hozman

After she was diagnosed with breast cancer, Suellen Hozman felt little kinship with the inspiring, uplifting stories of breast cancer survival she encountered at most support groups and fundraisers. Hozman's own cancer treatment was painful and traumatic, but she felt little need to enter the "cancer competition," as she saw it.

Instead of talking publicly about her struggles with cancer, Hozman retreated, facing treatments matter-of-factly and, mostly, in silence. Her survival story is bitter, full of loneliness and anger rather than inspiration, but, as she argues, she is far from the only person who has survived cancer this way.

Suellen Hozman was a registered nurse prior to her retirement. Having survived breast cancer, she is as of 2007 a sculptor and photographer living in Michigan.

The audience huddles at round tables in the big room. The tables are set; there are cloth napkins. There's a raised platform for the speakers and fundraisers. Then it begins. Quiche, fruit, and pep talks. First, the executive director of Making Strides Against Breast Cancer gives the I'm-so-moved-at-the-outpouring-of-support speech. Next, time is given to the businesses that pledged the largest amount of money to the organization. You'd recognize the names. They're the big employers in your community. Finally, there is the survivor.

She is upbeat, grateful, and hopeful—despite the chemo, radiation, and surgery. She's in her 30s. She has small children. She smiles when she describes how much she loves her doctors and nurses. She says that she's a better person now.

Suellen Hozman, "The Other Cancer Story," *American Journal of Nursing*, November 2005. Reproduced by permission.

She doesn't describe the indigestible images of cancer: nonanesthetized injections at the tumor site, breasts and nipples inflamed from radiation. The audience finds her inspiring; their quiche goes down just fine.

I admire the survivor. I'm happy for her strength and spirit. I feel terrible that she got breast cancer at such a young age, before her children were grown. As a single parent, I asked not to die until my boys were grown. I got that wish.

But there's another side to the cancer story.

Joining the Cancer Club

I joined the club on May 8, 2000. I was at my mother's apartment when I called my doctor's office for my results. I was shocked. So was my mother. "And you eat vegetables," she said. "You never know." At 86, a first-generation American born of Russian Jewish parents, my mother knew something about life's absence of guarantees.

From the beginning, my close friends and immediate family were wonderful. After the diagnosis, my good friend Robert drove me to my son Joshua's house. Joshua, who fills a doorway, held me, wept, and said, "Mom, we're doing this together."

But it was different with acquaintances. With them, conversations would go like this:

"I have breast cancer."

"Oh, I know an aunt (sister, wife, friend, coworker) who had breast cancer."

How should I have responded? Need I have asked to hear their stories and braced myself to learn about the dead ones? Is this a breast cancer competition? I wanted to ask, "Do you want me to feel good about my diagnosis just because I'm still alive?" It stunned me that coworkers and acquaintances found it so hard to simply listen. Why was it so uncommon for someone to say, "I'm sorry for your pain"?

Failing to Find Support

I tried a local support group. The stories from the young women dealing with second and third occurrences were too brutal. It reminded me of my childhood neighbors, Holocaust survivors with numbers on their arms. It felt like breast cancer genocide. I made it to only one meeting.

So I became private, no longer sharing my diagnosis in casual interactions. I needed all my emotional reserves to survive the damn treatments. The cancer never hurt until I agreed to get cured.

There's no cookie-cutter treatment for breast cancer. Mine was mine: two surgeries, six weeks of radiation, and thirteen months of tamoxifen [a breast cancer drug that stops tumor growth and spreading]. It caused vocal chord disturbance, resurrection of irritable bowel syndrome, first-ever asthma symptoms, nonstop vaginal yeast infections, and atrophic vaginitis [thinning of the lining of the vagina]. Tamoxifen was killing me. But no alternate drug options were made available, even after I asked my oncologist. So I simply stopped taking it.

A Lonely Battle

But I never stopped working. I received radiation at 7:15 A.M. and was usually at work by 8. No one brought me food, mowed my lawn, offered to take me out, or brought me a candle. As a single parent since 1978, I've come to be known as independent and self-sufficient. I didn't ask for help; I just continued on, day by day. There are millions like me out there who didn't win the Tour de France after cancer.

So I'm not a better person as a result of cancer. I'm unattractively hypochondriacal [being obsessed with imagined physical complaints]. I feel a pain in my groin after my daily walk and wonder if it's the first sign of pelvic cancer. Cancer wasn't my epiphany. It was painful and lonely. I'm the other cancer story. And I'm still alive.

Remember Me as a Writer, Not a Survivor

Donna Trussell

Following her diagnosis with Stage III ovarian cancer at the age of forty-eight, writer Donna Trussell discovered that she had lost her passion for writing. Discouraged by the prognosis for ovarian cancer patients, Trussell found it nearly impossible to remain motivated enough to submit her writing for publication, certain that she would not live long enough to see it in print.

After surviving cancer for three years, however, Trussell rediscovered her love of writing and became determined to preserve her identity as a successful writer, not just as a cancer survivor. Her essay describes her gradual process through anger, depression, activism, and finally the recollection of her pre-cancer writing self.

Donna Trussell is a poet, essayist, film critic, and short story writer whose writing has appeared in newspapers and literary journals. She lives in Kansas City. To read samples of Trussell's writing, including the poem "The Oncologist and Her Ghosts" and "Everything Changed," an essay about her cancer diagnosis, visit her Web site: http://www.donnatrussell.com.

M Y ONCOLOGIST'S NURSE found out I was a writer. "You must keep a journal!" she said. "I have nothing to say on this subject. I have no comment."

"But it could help other women."

"I don't care about them," I said.

That was true enough in the first few months after I discovered I had ovarian cancer, but what I didn't say was that writing had long ago lost its glow. I often found myself remembering Marcel Duchamp's last painting, "Tu m'" ("You Bore Me"). Even my work as a film critic for the local alternative paper suffered. I was often tempted to write, "Go see it and decide for yourself."

If typing, revising and mailing literary manuscripts was tedious before, it seemed absurd now. Statistics gave me a 30 percent chance of living five years.

Expecting the Worst

Breast cancer's five-year survival rate is more than 80 percent, so it should not have surprised me when I thumbed through a list of local support groups and found plenty for breast and none for ovarian. Then it occurred to me: of course, they're all dead!

Not that death was a stranger. My poems tended toward death, death, death, pet death, death, sex, love, death.

Still, I was unprepared for just how unprepared I was to face my diagnosis. I would say it hit me like a train except that would describe the violence and not the despair, which was more like the embrace of a frozen corpse.

Ovarian cancer recurs frequently, and I could not shake the belief that no matter how well I'd done so far, I would not live long. Hoping for an edge, I asked the doctor about my cell type.

"Clear cell," she said.

"How does that affect my prognosis?"

"It doesn't," she said.

I soon learned she was a voice in the wilderness. Every researcher on the planet, it seemed, thought clear cell the worst ovarian malignancy.

A Reluctant Activist

Panicked, I found an online group of "ovca sisters" and asked if they'd heard any good news about clear cell. In a word: nope. But they were glad I'd found them. Every day I read messages from women who shared my limbo existence. Those of us in remission could imagine our futures in the grim posts of the ill.

Some members gave up good-paying jobs to become activists. Ah, civic duty. I just couldn't hear the call. However, I did have a standing invitation from the local paper to write on any subject. I suggested a personal essay in time for Ovarian Cancer Awareness Month.

The next day an editor phoned. "I hear you're writing a piece for us." "I already wrote it," I said. My productivity surprised even me. On Sept. 2, 2002, almost one year after my surgery, "Everything Changed" ran in the *Kansas City Star*. I got calls and letters.

I helped form a local support group, but I warned the members I was not a "group person." I might have only months to live, so I had to be choosy. Only one project really appealed to me. On the Internet I found cancer poems and asked friends to read them at an event, "Women, Interrupted: An Evening of Music and Poetry Dedicated to Cancer Survivors and Loved Ones Lost."

Returning to Writing

The event was a success but I wouldn't remain an activist long. Contrarian that I am, I started an argument.

The Pulitzer Prize-winning play "Wit," about an English professor dying of ovarian cancer, was, in my opinion, one long I-admire-your-bravery speech. So what if it put ovarian cancer on the map?

My ovca sisters were appalled. I was a traitor. But I was thinking like a writer again. I even wrote a new poem, titled "The Oncologist and Her Ghosts."

On the anniversary of my diagnosis, I followed the lead of another group member—I sent my oncologist a gift with a card that read, "Do you remember what you were doing three years ago today? I do. You were saving my life."

It was beginning to look like I would have to learn how to live again instead of how to die. I decided to apply to the Bread Loaf Writers' Conference in Vermont, where I had won a scholarship in 1989.

Bread Loaf required 10 poems, and I couldn't just trot out my sleek, muscular, published warhorses. I had to write new poems and quickly whip them into shape. It was a humbling experience, but I got the application in the mail.

My ovca sisters don't hear from me much anymore. They probably think I'm in denial, that I believe I'm cured. They couldn't be more wrong.

Cancer may take me yet—next month, next year or in 10 years. Whenever death comes, my obituary will not call me a cancer survivor. I will die, simply, a writer.

Two Breast Cancer Survival Stories

Patti Balwanz, Kim Carlos, Jennifer Johnson,
and Jana Peters

Once a month, four twenty-something professional women met for lunch at Nordstrom's Café in Kansas City. For these four women, all of whom were undergoing treatment for breast cancer, their regularly scheduled luncheons became an invaluable source of friendship and support during their illness.

In the following selection, two of the friends—Jana Peters and Kim Carlos—discuss the lessons they learned during their long battles with breast cancer. Both of the women were inspired by their cancer not only to make key changes in their professional and personal lives but also to become passionate advocates for breast cancer research and awareness. Both women argue that living with a life-threatening illness has actually made their lives richer and more meaningful.

Kim Carlos is as of 2007 cancer-free and living in Kansas City with her husband and young son. She operates a consulting and advocacy business and makes frequent speaking appearances. Jana Peters founded the Ribbons of Pink nonprofit organization, a foundation established to provide support for young women with breast cancer. Following a courageous eight-year battle against breast cancer, Jana died in December of 2006.

Jana

My surgeon warned me: "Cancer will not change you. It will amplify who you already were before you were diagnosed." So if you're a "glass-half-empty" person before cancer, you'll have a negative experience. But if you saw your world through rose-colored glasses before cancer, then you'll find some rose-tinged moments during and after your diagnosis.

I was viewing life through rose-colored glasses before my diagnosis. My career was developing in a field I loved. I was recently engaged. Quite simply, I was happy. My glass was half full then, and has only become more full during the experience. Let me explain.

At the time of this writing, I have lived for eight years since the fateful day I first felt the lemon-drop lump in my breast. During those years, I went through one lumpectomy and biopsy and was diagnosed with Stage I multifocal breast cancer. I had a mastectomy with no reconstruction, four rounds of high-dose chemotherapy, hair loss, two wigs, a fake boob, and a toxic, painful reaction to chemotherapy.

I also had one fabulous wedding and honeymoon, and I have celebrated seven wedding anniversaries since.

When cancer spread to my bones and I was diagnosed with Stage IV cancer, a drama-packed visit to the M. D. Anderson Cancer Center brought me the disconcerting message that I had a 20 percent chance of surviving for five years. A Port-a-Cath was permanently inserted, and I began the first of what now totals more than sixty-two consecutive Aredia [used to treat high blood calcium levels] monthly infusions. Zoladex [a drug that reduces breast cancer symptoms] put me into premature menopause with thousands of hot flashes and forty pounds of weight gain. A prophylactic [preventive] mastectomy prior to reconstructive surgery led to the discovery of more cancer in my chest-wall muscle. After thirty-three zaps of radiation, I completed my bilateral breast reconstruction with saline implants.

The reality that this disease can be fatal became undeniable after my dear "chemo friend" Patti died from it.

In the midst of all of these events, it would have been easy to become a glass-half-empty person. But my surgeon was right: Breast cancer amplified who I was prior to being diagnosed, which is why I can say that life is still good!

Foremost, it's because my faith has grown and I am finally beginning to understand my purpose in life. Simply, I am here to serve God. From Patti's writings, it's obvious that she lived her life to glorify God. I never fully understood it, though, until months after she was gone.

Now I wake up each morning realizing that this day is a gift and there are no promises for tomorrow. One day will be my last day, but even that day will be good because I believe I will be going somewhere even better.

Chris and I have packed more into our seven years of marriage than many couples do in their entire lifetimes. We have honeymooned in Maui, traveled extensively around the United States, gone on Caribbean cruises, swum with dolphins, vacationed in Oahu and Kauai, and bought a timeshare in the desert. We built a new house in the suburbs, then quit our jobs in the Midwest and moved to San Francisco in pursuit of an action-packed life in a city I always dreamt of living in. And, we have two sweet cats who greet us when we come home each day. Each day, our love grows stronger. We have a solid relationship I never imagined possible.

My Pink Tattoo

In celebration of my fifth year of survival, I had a pink ribbon tattooed onto my ankle. My parents were shocked and disappointed. "Some day you'll regret it," they warned.

I hope I do live long enough to regret having a tattoo. Or maybe I will not regret it, and instead will be showing it off to my fellow gray-hairs at the retirement center when I am ninety. By then, it will look like a small blob on wrinkled skin, but I will proudly explain how, sixty-odd years earlier, it was a badge I wore to remind myself of what I had gone through. And that is what it is—a badge.

My surgical scars are also badges and reminders, but I don't often look at them any more, and they are even beginning to fade. My ankle tattoo is something I can easily glance at. It visibly reminds me that I must never take a day for granted. It reminds me that hope and faith carried me through one set of difficult times and will carry me through again when I need special strength and courage.

Today, I sometimes forget about the disease that could some day take my life. Of course, I think about it when I go for my monthly infusions and lab work. I think about it when I am lying on a CT [computed tomography; an imaging method] scan table, hoping nothing is found. I think about it when I get my prescriptions refilled. But I no longer think about it every day.

Making Lists

To live my life as I believe God wants me to, I have created two lists. The first is what I absolutely must do before I die. The second is a list of what I want to do before I die. I may not make it all the way through the second list, but I'm going to try.

The first list is more difficult and holds challenges. It is, by far, more important. Some of the things I learned from Patti: "Living a life that glorifies God, making sure relationships in my life are right, and striving to fulfill my life's purpose."

The second list includes things such as my career aspirations and places I want to visit. It's much more "fun" and includes only things that really won't matter after I die.

A Mission to Help Others

I don't believe I went through all I have gone through to help just one person. I want to help as many people as possible. I hope to reach thousands of women and educate them about breast health. I want to help other young survivors. That's why I've spent countless hours working with several breast cancer organizations, including the one I founded in 1999, the Ribbons of Pink Foundation (ROP).

Inspiration for ROP came from two places. First, when I was diagnosed, there were no organizations that focused on young women with breast cancer. Second, fourteen months after my initial diagnosis, as I drove around an upscale shopping center, I saw brightly colored banners adorning each of the light posts around the parking lot. I had an idea. October is National Breast Cancer Awareness Month. Why not display giant pink ribbon banners on the light posts in October to promote breast cancer awareness?

After a few phone calls and meetings, the shopping center management agreed to fund half the banners if I could raise the rest of the money. With the help of my stepmom, we sold "advertising space" on specially designed tee shirts, and we raised several thousand dollars. We purchased banners, sold more tee shirts throughout October, and handed out breast cancer awareness information at tables set up in the shopping center. The remaining proceeds were donated to the American Cancer Society.

When I saw one hundred light posts, each alternating with a black or white background and a giant pink ribbon, I became teary eyed. The black banners were in memory of those who had died from breast cancer. The white banners represented hope and survivorship.

Starting a Nonprofit

Soon the local media started interviewing me, and that gave me the idea of starting a nonprofit organization. The mission of ROP is to "Promote Breast Health & Support Young Breast Cancer Survivors." After more news stories, the ball began to roll, and it has continued to gain momentum. In 2005, ROP became a Fund of the Greater Kansas City Community Foundation and is no longer a free-standing organization. I am so proud that after many years of fund-raising efforts, ROP was able to set up a fund to provide grants to organizations that meet our mission for many years to come. This is a dream come true, and I am grateful to everyone who helped realize this dream. (For more information, visit www.ribbonsof pink.org.)

My involvement in ROP and other breast cancer organizations has made me aware of the importance of volunteering and donating financially to such charities. I also now make an effort to purchase items with pink ribbons that support breast cancer programs and reseach. . . .

Having faced several disease recurrences, I am not certain anymore that I'm going to win this battle against cancer. But I am not going to stop fighting. I have accepted that I am not in control of the disease—but I am in control of how I choose to deal with it. So I will continue the prescribed medical regimens. I will choose to have a positive attitude. And I will choose to live each day as if it were my last, because it could be. . . .

Kim

Many people who face a life-threatening disease will tell you later that it has changed their lives for the better. I am no exception. The lessons I learned by facing my own death from cancer, as well as from losing a dear friend and an aunt to the same disease, are lessons that most people don't learn until they're much older and wiser, if they learn them at all. I feel blessed to have such a great perspective on life at such a young age.

Breast cancer was the best teacher I ever had. After my diagnosis, I found strengths within that I didn't know I possessed. After hearing those fateful four words, "You have breast cancer," it was as if my entire life had flashed before my eyes. But not just the life I've already lived—also the life I was afraid I wouldn't be around to see. For me, surviving those private scary moments and being able to pull myself out of the depths of my own private hell made me a stronger person—a survivor! I made a conscious decision to go back to the doctor and fight this disease with all the strength I had. I chose to have all those surgeries and to put those poisonous drugs into my system to kill any stray cancer cells that might be floating around. I chose to concentrate on living, not the alternative. I looked at this journey as a major inconvenience in my life, and I tried to find the positive to help get me through.

Becoming an Advocate

Cancer taught me the importance of becoming an advocate; of asking the hard questions; of taking action and being proactive. I have learned it is important to be my own advocate and to take control of my own health and life. I realized that no one else was going to do it for me. I learned the importance of early detection—it saved my life. I learned to practice the three steps to breast health, namely, perform a monthly breast exam and get an annual clinical breast exam and an annual mammogram.

I made a list of questions and interviewed my doctors. I even took a tape recorder along. When one of my doctors did not answer my questions adequately, I got a second opinion and ended up changing doctors. Don't be afraid to get a second opinion and even a third opinion. It's your body and your life.

Cancer also taught me . . . to accept help. This was a hard lesson because I'd always been the one giving help. But with no family in town, and my firefighter husband on twenty-four-hour shifts, I knew I couldn't keep up with our Energizer Bunny son while in chemotherapy. So I let my friends bring meals, baby-sit, and even clean my toilets. It helped them to know they were helping me.

Learning to Let Go

This is what I tell people: "Hey, thanks to breast cancer, I got rid of my mommy fat with a tummy tuck, and I got a breast lift, too!" Humor is a healing factor. Precancer, I was uptight and serious; cancer taught me to laugh at myself and have more fun.

Prior to breast cancer, I was running the rat race, trying to be a super-mom, super-employee, super-aunt—trying to be just plain super. Looking back, I realize that I wasn't having much fun. I was so focused on my Palm Pilot that I forgot to enjoy life. Now I try to enjoy every minute. It's about making choices. Who cares if the house is a little dusty?

Before cancer, I had my life planned out—my five-year plan; my ten-year plan; my retirement plan. I had my entire life planned. Breast cancer taught me that, as John Lennon said, "Life is what happens while we're making other plans." We're not always in control.

The reality is that life is about uncertainty. But after a breast cancer diagnosis, it seemed that uncertainty was taking over my life. Those first few weeks of my diagnosis were very frustrating because I was not in control. For once in my life, I didn't have control over the situation. I couldn't put the bad days down in my Palm Pilot and schedule around them. Uncertainty seemed to surround me. I was uncertain about what the future held for me. However, none of us knows what the future holds, so we need to live for today. This wasn't an easy lesson to learn or to accept. I learned that life is precious and fragile and that you'd better make today count.

As a focused, driven person, precancer, I'd set a goal, reach it, and immediately move on to the next. Now my goal is to live a balanced life, which means spending time on things that are important—things I feel passionate about—and also leaving time to enjoy the unplanned moment.

For instance, one day as I was leaving a meeting, it started to rain. Other women were getting rides to their cars so that they wouldn't get wet, but I said, "No thanks." I walked to the car without an umbrella, enjoying the rain and not worrying about having a bad hair day.

New Freedoms

I also learned to make time for myself—something that I didn't do enough of precancer. I read *People* and *US Weekly*; I get pedicures and manicures; I spend more time with family and friends; I travel more; I work less; and I say no more often.

Breast cancer gave me a newfound sense of freedom. I am not afraid of taking risks and of making mistakes. I've decided that I don't want to look back on my life when I'm eighty and, instead of seeing all the risks I took and goals I achieved, see excuses and reasons why I didn't try. I don't want to have any regrets. Life is too short.

Two years after my diagnosis, I realized that I had to follow my own advice. So I quit my high-paying law firm job to follow my passion. Since I was the chief breadwinner in our family (as I mentioned in an earlier chapter, my husband followed his own passion and hung up his business suit for a firefighter's suit), this decision carried some risk. However, it was a risk that I was willing to take. That's because cancer taught me to be less afraid of taking risks or of making mistakes. I am now making a difference, having fun, spending more time with family and friends, and earning a living at the same time.

As it did for the other Nordie Girls, breast cancer renewed my faith in God. My faith has been strengthened and I am now living each day as God's servant. Cancer helped me to see the big picture and realize that "the purpose of life is a life of purpose" (Robert Byrne).

A Renewed Commitment

Breast cancer reiterated to me that one person can make a difference. Although my parents taught me from an early age to give back to the community, my passion is even more focused as a result of my breast cancer. October, National Breast Cancer Awareness Month, will be filled with cancer awareness events for the rest of my life. I've had the honor through my breast cancer work to share the stage with governors, Miss America, and movie stars. For my advocacy efforts, I've been recognized nationally by Lifetime Television, *Self* magazine, and the Komen Foundation. However, for me, the most rewarding part has been helping other women when they're diagnosed with breast cancer. Through my "missionary" work of supporting newly diagnosed breast cancer patients and working with the Susan G. Komen Breast Cancer Foundation, the Young Survival Coalition, the American Cancer Society, the National Patient Advocate Foundation, and the many other great organizations for which I volunteer, I feel that I am making a difference. Margaret Mead said, "Never doubt that a small group of thoughtful committed citizens can change the world. Indeed, it is the only thing that ever has." Amen to that.

Making a Difference

My breast cancer diagnosis also made me become even more of an advocate, not just with breast cancer patients, but with policymakers. Although I had been involved with politics all my life, it was after my breast cancer diagnosis that I realized the true value of public policy and advocacy. The reality is that politics affects every one of us every day. As a person living with breast cancer, I understand that reality now more than ever. Breast cancer. It's a health issue, a family issue, a women's issue, and, yes, breast cancer is a political issue. Why?

Because every day elected officials and other key policymakers make decisions about breast health and breast cancer care. Every day, politicians make important decisions about how much funding will be devoted to breast cancer research and who will have access to quality cancer care. These are not theoretical decisions. Breast cancer policies debated at the federal, state, and local levels affect everyone. This realization has made me become even more of an advocate for breast cancer research, education, screening, and treatment, from the halls of Congress to the White Home, by getting involved with important public policy issues. I was very excited to be able to lead the Komen Champions for the Cure™ program for the Komen Kansas City Affiliate, and was even more honored when I was asked to join Komen's National Public Policy Advisory Council. Through these efforts, I feel I am using my talents and passion to help others. Each of us has a unique opportunity to become involved in public policy and shape not only the present but also the future. This ensures that those who come after us will be given the access and treatment they deserve.

For me, life is still amazingly good. I am living for the moment because tomorrow is never promised. I am not only surviving; I'm thriving.

Getting My Life Back

Lance Armstrong with Sally Jenkins

Perhaps the most famous cancer survivor is professional cyclist Lance Armstrong. In 1996, ranked as the number one cyclist in the world, Armstrong was diagnosed with testicular cancer, which had also spread to his lungs and his brain. Faced with nearly insurmountable odds, Armstrong made a full recovery and went on to win the Tour de France seven consecutive times from 1999 to 2005.

Armstrong's comeback was not an easy one, however, as this story makes clear. Following cancer treatments, Armstrong initially lost the will to succeed that had driven him to his earlier career achievements. He found himself questioning his motivation and giving in to setbacks and failures. Only when he got back on his bike and recommenced hard training did Armstrong rediscover his former self.

In addition to his remarkable sports accomplishments, Armstrong, now retired from cycling, founded the Lance Armstrong Foundation, a cancer education and advocacy group whose trademark yellow "LIVESTRONG" wristbands are worn by over 55 million people worldwide.

While I was sick, I told myself I'd never cuss again, never drink another beer again, never lose my temper again. I was going to be the greatest and the most clean-living guy you could hope to meet. But life goes on. Things change, intentions get lost. You have another beer. You say another cussword.

How do you slip back into the ordinary world? That was the problem confronting me after cancer, and the old saying, that you should treat each day as if it might be your last, was no help at all. The truth is, it's a nice sentiment, but in practice it doesn't work. If I lived only for the moment, I'd be a very amiable no-account with a perpetual three-day growth on my chin. Trust me, I tried it.

People think of my comeback as a triumph, but in the beginning, it was a disaster. When you have lived for an entire year terrified of dying, you feel like you deserve to spend the rest of your days on a permanent vacation. You can't, of course; you have to return to your family, your peers, and your profession. But a part of me didn't want my old life back.

We moved to Europe in January with the U.S. Postal [cycling] team. Kik [nickname of Kristin Richard, Armstrong's fiancé and future wife] quit her job, gave away her dog, leased her house, and packed up everything she owned. We rented an apartment in Cap Ferrat, halfway between Nice and Monaco, and I left her there alone while I went on the road with the team. A race wasn't an environment for wives and girlfriends. It was no different from the office; it was a job, and you didn't take your wife to the conference room.

Kristin was on her own in a foreign country, with no friends or family, and she didn't speak the language. But she reacted typically, by enrolling herself in a language-intensive French school, furnishing the apartment, and settling in as if it was a great adventure, with absolutely no sign of fear. Not once did she complain. I was proud of her.

My own attitude wasn't as good. Things weren't going so well for me on the road, where I had to adjust all over again to the hardships of racing through Europe. I had forgotten what it was like. The last time I'd been on the continent was on vacation with Kik, when we'd stayed in the best hotels and played tourists, but now it was back to the awful food, the bad beds in dingy road *pensions* [small hotels or boardinghouses], and the incessant travel. I didn't like it.

Deep down, I wasn't ready. Had I understood more about survivorship, I would have recognized that my comeback attempt was bound to be fraught with psychological problems. If I had a bad day, I had a tendency to say, "Well, I've just been through too much. I've been through three surgeries, three months of chemo, and a year of hell, and that's the reason I'm not riding well. My body is just never going to be the same." But what I really should have been saying was, "Hey, it's just a bad day."

I was riding with buried doubts, and some buried resentments too. I was making a fraction of my old salary, and I had no new endorsements. I sarcastically called it "an eighty-percent cancer tax." I'd assumed that the minute I got back on the bike and announced a comeback, corporate America would come knocking, and when they didn't, I blamed Bill [Bill Stopletos, Armstrong's agent]. I drove him nuts, constantly asking him why he wasn't bringing me any deals. Finally, we had a confrontation via phone—I was in Europe, he was back in Texas. I began complaining again that nothing was happening on the endorsement front.

"Look, I'll tell you what," Bill [Stapleton] said. "I'm going to find you a new agent. I'm not putting up with this anymore. I know you think I need this, but I don't. So I quit."

I paused and said, "Well, that's not what I want."

I stopped venting on Bill, but I still brooded about the fact that no one wanted me. No European teams wanted me, and corporate America didn't want me.

My first pro race in 18 months was the Ruta del Sol, a five-day jaunt through Spain. I finished 14th, and caused a stir, but I was depressed and uncomfortable. I was used to leading, not finishing 14th. Also, I hated the attention of that first race. I felt constrained by performance anxiety and distracted by the press circus, and I wished I could have just shown up unannounced and ridden without a word, fighting through my self-doubts anonymously. I just wanted to ride in the peloton [the main group in a road bicycle race] and get my legs back.

Two weeks later, I entered Paris-Nice, among the most arduous stage races outside of the Tour de France itself, an eight-day haul notorious for its wintry raw weather. Before the race itself was the "prologue," a time-trial competition. It was a seeding system of sorts; the results of the prologue would determine who rode at the front of the peloton. I finished in 19th place, not bad for a guy recovering from cancer, but I didn't see it that way. I was used to winning.

The next morning I woke up to a gray rain and blustering wind, and temperatures in the 30s. As soon as I opened my eyes I knew I didn't want to ride in that weather. I ate my breakfast morosely. I met with the team to discuss the strategy for the day, and we decided as a squad that if our team leader, George Hincapie, fell behind for any reason, we would all wait for him and help him catch up.

In the start area, I sat in a car trying to keep warm and thought about how much I didn't want to be there. When you start out thinking that way, things can't possibly get any better. Once I got out in the cold, my attitude just deteriorated. I sulked as I put on leg warmers and fought to keep some small patch of my skin dry.

We set off on a long, flat stage. The rain spit sideways, and a crosswind made it seem even colder than 35 degrees. There is nothing more demoralizing than a long flat road in the rain. At least on a climb your body stays a little bit warm because you have to work so hard, but on a flat road, you just get cold and wet to the bone. No shoe cover is good enough. No jacket is good enough. In the past, I'd thrived on being able to stand conditions that made everyone else crack. But not on this day.

Hincapie got a flat.

We all stopped. The peloton sped up the road away from us. By the time we got going again, we were 20 minutes behind the leaders, and in the wind it would take an hour of brutal effort for us to make up what we had lost. We rode off, heads down into the rain.

The crosswind cut through my clothes and made it hard to steady the bike as I churned along the side of the road. All of a sudden, I lifted my hands to the tops of the handlebars. I straightened up in my seat, and I coasted to the curb.

I pulled over. I quit. I abandoned the race. I took off my number. I thought, *This is not how I want to spend my life, freezing and soaked and in the gutter.*

Frankie Andreu was right behind me, and he remembers how I looked as I rose up and swung off the road. He could tell by the way I sat up that I might not race again for a while—if ever. Frankie told me later that his thought was "He's done."

When the rest of the team arrived back at the hotel at the end of the stage, I was packing. "I quit," I told Frankie. "I'm not racing anymore, I'm going home." I didn't care if my teammates understood or not. I said goodbye, slung my bag over my shoulder, and took off.

The decision to abandon had nothing to do with how I felt physically. I was strong. I just didn't want to be there. I simply didn't know if cycling through the cold and the pain was what I wanted to do for the rest of my life. . . .

[After returning to the United States] Bill patiently manipulated me into holding off on a retirement announcement. With every complication he summoned up, he bought more time. At the very least I couldn't retire before Ride for the Roses, he said, and that wasn't until May.

Finally, Bill wore me down, I told him I would wait to announce anything. But in the meantime, I decided I would take a few days off.

My Postal team was patient. Thom Weisel offered to wait. But a few days off turned into a week, and then a week turned into a month. I didn't even unpack my bike. It sat in its bag in the garage, collecting dust.

I was a bum. I played golf every day, I water-skied, I drank beer, and I lay on the sofa and channel-surfed.

I went to Chuy's for Tex-Mex, and violated every rule of my training diet. Whenever I came home from Europe, it was a tradition for me to stop at Chuy's straight from the airport, no matter how jet-lagged I was, and order a burrito with tomatillo sauce and a couple of margaritas or Shiner Bocks. Now I was eating practically every meal there. I never intended to deprive myself again; I'd been given a second chance and I was determined to take advantage of it.

But it wasn't fun. It wasn't lighthearted or free or happy. It was forced. I tried to re-create the mood I'd shared with Kik on our European vacation, but this time, things were different, and I couldn't understand why. The truth was, I felt ashamed. I was filled with self-doubt and embarrassed by what I'd done in Paris-Nice. *Son, you never quit.* But I'd quit.

I was behaving totally out of character, and the reason was survivorship. It was a classic case of "Now what?" I'd had a job and a life, and then I got sick, and it turned my life upside-down, and when I tried to go back to my life I was disoriented, nothing was the same—and I couldn't handle it.

I hated the bike, but I thought, *What else am I going to do? Be a coffee boy in an office?* I didn't exactly feel like a champ at much else. I didn't know what to do, so for the moment, I just wanted to escape, and that's what I did. I evaded my responsibilities.

I know now that surviving cancer involved more than just a convalescence of the body. My mind and my soul had to convalesce, too.

No one quite understood that—except for Kik. She kept her composure when she had every right to be distraught and furious with me for pulling the rug out from under her. While I was out playing golf every day, she was homeless, dogless, and jobless, reading the classifieds and wondering how we were going to support ourselves. My mother sympathized with what she was going through. She would call us, ask to speak with Kik, and say, "How are *you* doing?"

But after several weeks of the golf, the drinking, the Mexican food, Kik decided it was enough—somebody had to try to get through to me. One morning we were sitting outside on the patio having coffee. I put down my cup and said, "Well, okay, I'll see you later. It's my tee time."

"Lance," Kik said, "what am *I* doing today?"

"What do you mean?"

"You didn't ask me what I was going to do today. You didn't ask me what I wanted to do, or if I minded if you played golf. You just told me what you were going to do. Do you care what I'm doing?"

"Oh, sorry," I said.

"What am I doing today?" she said. "What am I doing? Tell me that."

I was silent. I didn't know what to say.

"You need to decide something," she told me. "You need to decide if you are going to retire for real, and be a golf-playing, beer-drinking, Mexican-food-eating slob. If you are, that's fine. I love you, and I'll marry you anyway. But I just need to know, so I can get myself together and go back on the street, and get a job to support your golfing. Just tell me.

"But if you're not going to retire, then you need to stop eating and drinking like this and being a bum, and you need to figure it out, because you are deciding by not deciding, and that is so un-Lance. It is just not you. And I'm not quite sure who you are right now. I love you anyway, but you need to figure something out." . . .

Kik and Stapleton and [Chris] Carmichael [an advisor] and Och [team manager Jim Ochowicz] conspired against me, talking constantly behind my back about how to get me back on the bike. I continued to say that I was retiring, but as the days wore on, I began to waver. Bill persuaded me to commit to one last race, the U.S. Pro Championships, which would be held in Philadelphia in May.

Chris Carmichael flew to Austin. He took one look in my garage, at the bike still in its carrying bag, and shook his head. Chris felt like Kik did, that I needed to make a conscious decision about whether I belonged back on the bike. "You're alive again, and now you need to get back to living," he repeated. But he knew I wasn't ready to commit to another full-scale comeback yet, so the surface excuse he gave for coming to Austin was simply to put together a training plan for the U.S. Championships. Also, the second Ride for the Roses was coming up, and the race would be a criterium [a bike race on a short course] around downtown Austin requiring that I be at least minimally fit. "You can't go out like this," Chris said, gesturing at my body. "You don't want to embarrass your foundation."

Chris insisted that regardless of what I decided about retirement, I needed an eight- to ten-day intensive training camp to get back to form. . . .

I began to enjoy the single-mindedness of training [in Boone, North Carolina], riding hard during the day and holing up in the cabin in the evenings. I even appreciated the awful weather. It was as if I was going back to Paris-Nice and staring the elements that had defeated me in the eye. What had cracked me in Paris were the cold, wet conditions, but now I took satisfaction in riding through them, the way I'd used to.

Toward the end of the camp, we decided to ride Beech Mountain. Chris knew exactly what he was doing when he suggested it, because there was a time when I owned that mountain. It was a strenuous 5,000-foot climb with a snow-capped summit, and it had been the crucial stage in my two

Tour Du Pont victories. I remembered laboring on up the mountainside with crowds lined along the route, and how they had painted my name across the road: "Go Armstrong."

We set out on yet another cold, raining, foggy day with a plan to ride a 100-mile loop before we returned and undertook the big finishing ascent of Beech Mountain. Chris would follow in a car, so we could load the bikes up on the rack after we reached the summit and drive back to the cabin for dinner.

We rode and rode through a steady rain, for four hours, and then five. By the time we got to the foot of Beech, I'd been on the bike for six hours, drenched. But I lifted myself up out of the saddle and propelled the bike up the incline, leaving Bob Roll [Tour de France cyclist] behind.

As I started up the rise, I saw an eerie sight: the road still had my name painted on it.

My wheels spun over the washed-out old yellow and white lettering. I glanced down between my feet. It said, faintly, *Viva Lance.*

I continued upward, and the mountain grew steeper. I hammered down on the pedals, working hard, and felt a small bloom of sweat and satisfaction, a heat under my skin almost like a liquor blush. My body reacted instinctively to the climb. Mindlessly, I rose out of my seat and picked up the pace. Suddenly, Chris pulled up behind me in the follow car, rolled down his window, and began driving me on. "Go, go, go!" he yelled. I glanced back at him. *"Allez Lance, allez, allez!"* he yelled. I mashed down on the pedals, heard my breath grow shorter, and I accelerated.

That ascent triggered something in me. As I rode upward, I reflected on my life, back to all points, my childhood, my early races, my illness, and how it changed me. Maybe it was the primitive act of climbing that made me confront the issues I'd been evading for weeks. It was time to quit stalling, I realized. *Move,* I told myself. *If you can still move, you aren't sick.*

I looked again at the ground as it passed under my wheels, at the water spitting off the tires and the spokes turning round. I saw more faded painted letters, and I saw my washed-out name: *Go Armstrong.*

As I continued upward, I saw my life as a whole. I saw the pattern and the privilege of it, and the purpose of it, too. It was simply this: I was meant for a long, hard climb.

I approached the summit. Behind me, Chris could see in the attitude of my body on the bike that I was having a change of heart. Some weight, he sensed, was simply no longer there.

Lightly, I reached the top of the mountain. I cruised to a halt. Chris put the car in park and got out. We didn't talk about what had just happened. Chris just looked at me, and said, "I'll put your bike on top of the car."

"No," I said. "Give me my rain jacket. I'm riding back."

I was restored. I was a bike racer again. Chris smiled and got back in the car.

Organizations to Contact

The editors have compiled the following list of organizations concerned with the issues debated in this book. The descriptions are derived from materials provided by the organizations. All have publications or information available for interested readers. The list was compiled on the date of publication of the present volume; the information provided here may change. Be aware that many organizations take several weeks or longer to respond to inquiries, so allow as much time as possible.

American Brain Tumor Association
2720 River Rd., Des Plaines, IL   60018
(847) 827-9910 • fax: (847) 827-9918
e-mail: info@abta.org
Web site: http://hope.abta.org

Founded in 1973, the American Brain Tumor Association is an independent fundraising organization that provides research money to scientists investigating brain tumor treatment and prevention in the United States and Canada. Publications include "A Primer of Brain Tumors," listings of support groups, and patient information on various treatment options. Founded by a woman who lost her young daughter to brain cancer, the organization also offers extensive resources especially for young people and their families, including a separate kids' Web site and a DVD, "Alex's Journey."

American Cancer Society (ACS)
PO Box 22718, Oklahoma City, OK   73123-1718
(800) ACS-2345
e-mail: encic@cancer.org
Web site: www.cancer.org

The American Cancer Society has state offices and more than 3,400 local chapters. The society funds research, promotes educational programs, and advocates for cancer patients and their families. Their Web site includes information on volunteering, links to fundraising and donation opportunities, and patient education information. Publications include *Couples Confronting Cancer*, *Our Mom Has Cancer*, and *The Cancer Atlas*.

Cancer*Care*
275 Seventh Ave., New York, NY   1000-6708
(212) 712–8400 • fax: (212) 712–8495
e-mail: info@cancercare.org
Web site: www.cancercare.org

Cancer*Care* provides free, professional support services to people affected by cancer. Their Web site offers several online support groups, including ones for young adults with cancer and for caregivers. In addition, Cancer*Care* provides telephone and face-to-face counseling in both individual and group settings. Cancer*Care* also offers educational workshops via telephone, as well as a variety of Connect brochures covering these educational topics.

Candlelighters Childhood Cancer Foundation
PO Box 498, Kensington, MD   20895–0498
(800) 366–2223 • fax: (301) 962–3521
e-mail: staff@candlelighters.org
Web site: www.candlelighters.org

Founded in 1970 by parents of children with cancer, Candlelighters offers support for children currently battling cancer and their families, as well as for survivors of childhood cancers and for those who have lost a child to cancer. The organization publishes several picture books, free for children diagnosed with cancer, as well as educational materials aimed at their families. The Candlelighters Web site provides dozens of links to organizations providing financial and legal assistance to families dealing with childhood cancer.

Damon Runyon Cancer Research Foundation
675 Third Ave., 25th Floor, New York, NY   10017

(877) 7CANCER
e-mail: info@drcrf.org
Web site: www.drcrf.org

The Damon Runyon Cancer Research Foundation has been committed to supporting emerging research in the field of cancer treatment and prevention for over sixty years. The foundation offers research grants to young scientists, and 100 percent of its direct donations go directly to its scientific award programs. Its administrative costs are covered by a variety of fundraising efforts, including an innovative program through which the organization resells prime tickets to Broadway shows. Its events also include theater benefits and fundraising climbs in Aspen, Colorado, and in Chicago's Sears Tower.

Gilda's Club Worldwide
222 Eighth Ave., Ste. 1402, New York, NY   10001
(888) GILDA-4-U
e-mail: info@gildasclub.org
Web site: www.gildasclub.org

The mission of Gilda's Club (named for comedian Gilda Radner, who died from ovarian cancer in 1989) is "to provide meeting places where men, women, and children living with cancer and their families and friends join with others to build emotional and social support as a supplement to medical care." Through support groups, lectures, and other networking opportunities, all held in comfortable, homelike settings, Gilda's club seeks to connect people living with cancer. Its newsletter, *GildaGram*, is distributed twice a year.

Intercultural Cancer Council
1709 Dryden, Ste. 1025, Houston, TX   77030
(713) 798–4617 • fax: (713) 798–6222
e-mail: icc@bcm.edu
Web site: www.iccnetwork.org

Sponsored by the Baylor College of Medicine, the Intercultural Cancer Council (ICC) works to alleviate the unequal impact of cancer on racial and ethnic minorities as well as medically underserved populations in the United States. It works to distribute educational materials to these populations, to make clinical trials and experimental treatments more equitably distributed, and to lobby on behalf of its constituency with policy makers and the healthcare industry. The ICC's motto is "Speaking with One Voice," and its newsletter, *The Voice*, is distributed electronically on a quarterly basis.

Lance Armstrong Foundation

PO Box 161150, Austin, TX 78716–1150
(512) 236–8820
Web site: www.livestrong.org

Many people are aware of the Lance Armstrong Foundation through the prevalence of its trademark yellow "LIVESTRONG" wristbands, worn by 55 million people worldwide and available through the Web site in exchange for a small donation. Donations go to support the ongoing efforts of cancer survivors as well as to fund testicular cancer research. Founded by Tour de France winner Lance Armstrong, a cancer survivor himself, the foundation also sponsors a series of fundraising bike rides across the United States.

Leukemia and Lymphoma Society

1311 Mamaroneck Ave., White Plains, NY 10605
(800) 955–4572 • fax: (914) 949–6691
e-mail: infocenter@leukemia-lymphoma.org
Web site: www.lls.org

Dedicated to fighting blood cancers such as leukemia, lymphoma, Hodgkin's disease, myeloma, and others, the Leukemia and Lymphoma Society has raised more than $483 million in research funding since its founding in 1949. The society publishes numerous fact sheets and pamphlets on blood cancers (available for free via the Web site) and also holds a series of workshops across the United States each year. The Leukemia and Lymphoma Society sponsors and participates in dozens of fundraising events annually. Its "Team in Training," the world's largest endurance sports training program, helps train athletes for marathons, triathlons, and cycling events in exchange for a commitment to fundraising.

National Coalition for Cancer Surviorship
1010 Wayne Ave., Ste. 770, Silver Spring, MD   20910
(301) 650–9127 • fax: (301) 565–9670
e-mail: info@canceradvocacy.org
Web site: www.canceradvocacy.org

This lobbying group, founded and sustained by cancer survivors, advocates for quality cancer care at the federal level. Its programs include Cancer Advocacy Now!, a grassroots advocacy network that aims to involve cancer survivors across the country in bringing cancer issues to the attention of lawmakers. Its online "Cancer Survival Toolbox" is a practical, comprehensive resource (available in English, Spanish, and Chinese) for helping cancer survivors and caregivers make good decisions during treatment and beyond.

Prostate Cancer Foundation
1250 Fourth St., Santa Monica, CA   90401
(800) 757–2873 • fax: (310) 570–4701
e-mail: info@prostatecancerfoundation.org
Web site: www.prostatecancerfoundation.org

The world's largest organization dedicated to supporting prostate cancer research, the Prostate Cancer Foundation also advocates for greater federal funding for this type of research. In addition to its twice-yearly newsletter, *Focus*, the foundation also publishes several books, including *An Introduction to Prostate Cancer, Nutrition and Prostate Cancer*, and *The Taste for Living Cookbook*.

Skin Cancer Foundation
245 Fifth Ave., Ste. 1403, New York, NY   10016
(212) 725-5176 • fax: (212) 725-5751
e-mail: info@skincancer.org
Web site: www.skincancer.org

Skin cancer is the world's most common cancer, affecting over a million Americans each year. The Skin Cancer Foundation is the only philanthropic organization solely devoted to raising funds and awareness for this prevalent type of cancer. The foundation sponsors educational programs, funds research, and sponsors public service announcements about sun safety and skin cancer prevention. Its publications include numerous posters and brochures, an annual journal, and the books *Play It Safe in the Sun* (for children) and *Sun Sense*.

Susan G. Komen for the Cure

5005 LBJ Fwy., Ste. 250, Dallas, TX   75244
(800) IM-AWARE • fax: (972) 855-1605
e-mail: info@komen.org
Web site: www.komen.org

Founded in 1982 by Nancy Brinker, whose sister Susan G. Komen died from breast cancer, Susan G. Komen for the Cure (formerly the Susan G. Komen Breast Cancer Foundation) has since become the world's largest grassroots network devoted to fighting and raising awareness of breast cancer. Supporting early detection, funding for therapies, and educational programs for women, the organization also sponsors the Komen Race for the Cure, the largest series of 5K races in the world, and partners with Avon in the annual series of Breast Cancer 3-Day fundraising walks. Its many publications are primarily fact sheets and brief pamphlets designed for physicians to distribute to their patients.

Walter Payton Cancer Fund

c/o Cancer Treatment Research Foundation
Schaumburg, IL   60173
(847) 342-7450
Web site: www.payton34.org

Founded in honor of legendary Chicago Bears running back Walter Payton, who died in 1999 from a rare form of liver cancer, the Walter Payton Cancer Fund contributes 100 percent of every fundraising dollar to cancer research. In addition to direct donations, the fund sponsors a Chicago-area 16,726-yard run (the distance equal to Payton's rushing record), with proceeds going to support hand-picked studies relevant to Payton's own fight against the disease.

Women's Cancer Network
230 W. Monroe, Ste. 2528, Chicago, IL   60606
(312) 578-1439
e-mail: info@thegcf.org
Web site: www.wcn.org

Sponsored by the Gynecologic Cancer Foundation and CancerSource, the Women's Cancer Network is an online resource for women and their families confronting reproductive cancers. The interactive, educational site offers information about various types of cancers affecting women, with answers to frequently asked questions, links to clinical trials, and advice on finding a physician. The Web site's "Wall of Hope" allows survivors to share their success stories with others. An extensive list of relevant books is also included on the site.

Web Sites

Association of Cancer Online Resources (ACOR)
http://www.acor.org

A valuable clearinghouse for online information related to cancer, ACOR's Web site offers more than 150 electronic mailing lists covering topics from pets with cancer to very rare forms of human cancer. It also offers listings of worthwhile Web sites devoted to the disease, as well as information on conditions, treatments, clinical trials, and publications.

Medline Plus: Cancer
http://www.nlm.nih.gov/medlineplus/cancer.html

This online resource, sponsored by the National Library of Medicine, is a good starting point for information on medical questions related to cancer. The site provides basic information on cancer as well as dozens of links to specific cancers, online references, interactive tutorials, and resources specific to various populations, from children to seniors.

National Cancer Institute
http://www.cancer.gov

This comprehensive medical resource is sponsored by the National Cancer Institute, the federal government's principal agency for cancer research and training. It offers background information on various types of cancer, a dictionary of cancer terms and drugs, and links to other organizations and Web sites providing education and support. NCI's Web site also lists clinical trials for cancer patients and offers a wide variety of free educational pamphlets available for ordering or downloading.

Oncolink
http://oncolink.upenn.edu

Maintained by the Abramson Cancer Center at the University of Pennsylvania, Oncolink bills itself as "The Web's first cancer resource." It provides up-to-date cancer news stories, links to resources about treating and coping with cancer, and information on a variety of conditions, ranging from introductory overviews to in-depth medical studies. The site also provides reviews of cancer books and videos as well as capsule summaries of recent journal articles in the field.

For Further Research

Books

Stephanie Byrum, *Knowing Stephanie*. Pittsburgh: University of Pittsburgh Press, 2003.

Jim Chastain, *I Survived Cancer but Never Won the Tour de France*. Tulsa, OK: Ha Publishing, 2007.

Andrea King Collier, *Still with Me: A Daughter's Journey of Love and Loss*. New York: Simon & Schuster, 2003.

Cathlyn Conway, *Ordinary Life: A Memoir of Illness*. Ann Arbor: University of Michigan Press, 2007.

The Creative Center, *Still Life: Documenting Cancer Survivorship*. New York: Umbrage, 2007.

Mina Dobic, *My Beautiful Life: How I Conquered Cancer Naturally*. Garden City Park, NY: Square One, 2007.

The Healing Project, *Voices of Lung Cancer*. Brooklyn, NY: LaChance, 2007.

Liz Holzemer, *Curveball: When Life Throws You a Brain Tumor*. Denver: Ghost Road Press, 2007.

Debra Jarvis, *It's Not About the Hair: And Other Certainties of Life and Cancer*. Seattle: Sasquatch, 2007.

Karen Karbo, *The Stuff of Life: A Daughter's Memoir*. New York: Bloomsbury, 2003.

Marisa Acocella Marchetto, *Cancer Vixen: A True Story*. New York: Knopf, 2006.

Jan Michael, *Flying Crooked: A Story of Accepting Cancer*. Berkeley, CA: Greystone, 2005.

Julianne S. Oktay, *Breast Cancer: Daughters Tell Their Stories*. New York: Haworth, 2005.

Eugene O'Kelly, *Chasing Daylight: How My Forthcoming Death Transformed My Life*. New York: McGraw-Hill, 2006.

Stephen Henry Schneider, *The Patient from Hell: How I Worked with My Doctors to Get the Best of Modern Medicine, and How You Can Too*. Cambridge, MA: Da Capo, 2005.

Maria Sirois, *Every Day Counts: Lessons in Love, Faith, and Resilience from Children Facing Illness*. New York: Walker, 2006.

Sean Swarner, *Keep Climbing: How I Beat Cancer and Reached the Top of the World*. New York: Atria, 2007.

Steve Will, *A Reason to Run: A Personal Journey Through Prostate Cancer and Other Manly Matters*. Spokane, WA: Ulyssian, 2006.

Adam Wishart, *One in Three: A Son's Journey into the History and Science of Cancer*. New York: Grove, 2007.

John Yow, *Why We Walk: The Inspirational Journey Toward a Cure for Breast Cancer*. Nashville, TN: Rutledge Hill, 2005.

Periodicals

Jonathan Alter, "My Life with Cancer," *Newsweek*, April 9, 2007.

Lance Armstrong, "We Have to Be Ruthless," *Newsweek*, April 9, 2007.

Caroline Bollinger, "Everything You Know About Cancer Is Wrong," *Prevention*, November 2005.

John Brant, "Following Terry Fox," *Runner's World*, January 2007.

Susan Brody, "Sister Survivors," *Ladies' Home Journal*, November 2006.

Arch Campbell, "The Comeback Kid," *Washingtonian*, March 2007.

Lisa Collier Cool, "Why Me?" *Reader's Digest*, July 2006.

Diane Di Costanzo, "What He Didn't Tell Her," *Good Housekeeping*, September 2006.

Tamika Felder, "What Cancer Taught Me About Living," *Essence*, July 2006.

Kinky Friedman, "Arrivederci, Melanoma," *Texas Monthly*, July 2004.

Gil Gaul, "Who Needs to Worry About Prostate Cancer?" *Men's Health*, July 2001.

Kimberly Goad, "A Boy's Life (After Cancer)," *Redbook*, November 2005.

Bernadine Healey, "Cancer and Me," *U.S. News & World Report*, April 9, 2007.

David Loxtercamp, "Hope: What the Doctor Ordered," *Commonwealth*, November 17, 2006.

Camille Peri, "The Road Back to Normal," *Ladies' Home Journal*, November 2005.

Curtis Pesman, "My Cancer Story," *Esquire*, May, June, and July 2001.

Erin Zammett Ruddy, "Battling Cancer While the World Watches," *Glamour*, November 2006.

Rene Syler, "Defending My Life," *O: The Oprah Magazine*, April 2007.

Marissa Janet Winokur, "My Battle with Cervical Cancer," *People*, February 5, 2007.

Index